Contents

Notes on the contributors

Keith Chantry is a teacher at Deighton Close School for Maladjusted Boys. Prior to this he was a Lecturer in Special Needs at Bishop Grosseteste College, Lincoln.

John Fitzpatrick is a Lecturer in Education in the Centre for Primary Education at the University of Manchester.

Dorothy Heathcote was for many years a Senior Lecturer in Drama and Education at the University of Newcastle on Tyne. She is currently enjoying a well-earned retirement. The other contributors to her chapter are past MEd students.

Tessa Roberts is a Senior Lecturer in the Department of Education at the University of Manchester.

Patricia Sanderson is a Lecturer in Physical Education and Dance at the University of Manchester.

Jean Turnbull is a Co-ordinator of Music for Brent, Greater London.

SPECIAL NEEDS IN ORDINARY SCHOOLS
General Editor: Peter Mittler

Encouraging Expression

Special Needs in Ordinary Schools

General editor: Peter Mittler
Associate editors: James Hogg, Peter Pumfrey, Tessa Roberts,
Colin Robson
Honorary advisory board: Neville Bennett, Marion Blythman,
George Cooke, John Fish, Ken Jones, Sylvia Phillips, Klaus Wedell,
Phillip Williams

Titles in this series

Meeting Special Needs in Ordinary Schools: An Overview

Concerning pre- and primary schooling:

Primary Schools and Special Needs: Policy, Planning and Provision
Communication in the Primary School
Developing Mathematical and Scientific Thinking in Young Children
Encouraging Expression: The Arts in the Primary Curriculum
Exploring the Environment
Special Needs in Pre-Schools

Concerning secondary schooling:

Secondary Schools for All Strategies for Special Needs
Humanities for All: Teaching Humanities in the Secondary School
Responding to Adolescent Needs: A Pastoral Care Approach
Science for All: Teaching Science in the Secondary School
Shut up! Communication in the Secondary School
Teaching Mathematics in the Secondary School

Concerning specific difficulties:

Children with Learning Difficulties
Children with Speech and Language Difficulties
Making a Difference: Teachers, Pupils and Behaviour
Physically Disabled Children
The Hearing Impaired Child
The Visually Handicapped Child in your Classroom

Encouraging Expression: The Arts in the Primary Curriculum

Edited by Tessa Roberts

CASSELL

Cassell Educational Limited
Artillery House
Artillery Row
London SW1P 1RT

First published 1988

British Library Cataloguing in Publication Data

Encouraging expression: the arts in the
   primary curriculum.—(Special needs in
   ordinary schools).
   1. Great Britain. Primary schools. Children
   with special educational needs. Curriculum
   subjects. Arts. Teaching
   I. Roberts, Tessa II. Series
   371.9'044'0941

ISBN: 0-304-31473-0

Phototypesetting by Activity Ltd., Salisbury, Wilts.
Printed and bound in Great Britain by Biddles Ltd.,
Guildford and King's Lynn

Last digit is print no: 9 8 7 6 5 4 3 2 1

Foreword: Towards education for all

AIMS

This series aims to support teachers as they respond to the challenge they face in meeting the needs of all children in their school, particularly those identified as having special educational needs.

Although there have been many useful publications in the field of special educational needs during the last decade, the distinguishing feature of the present series of volumes lies in their concern with specific areas of the curriculum in primary and secondary schools. We have tried to produce a series of conceptually coherent and professionally relevant books, each of which is concerned with ways in which children with varying levels of ability and motivation can be taught together. The books draw on the experience of practising teachers, teacher trainers and researchers and seek to provide practical guidelines on ways in which specific areas of the curriculum can be made more accessible to all children. The volumes provide many examples of curriculum adaptation, classroom activities, teacher–child interactions, as well as the mobilisation of resources inside and outside the school.

The series is organised largely in terms of age and subject groupings, but three 'overview' volumes have been prepared in order to provide an account of some major current issues and developments. Seamus Hegarty's *Meeting Special Needs in Ordinary Schools* gives an introduction to the field of special needs as a whole, whilst Sheila Wolfendale's *Primary Schools and Special Needs* and John Sayer's *Secondary Schools for All?* address issues more specifically concerned with primary and secondary schools respectively. We hope that curriculum specialists will find essential background and contextual material in these overview volumes.

In addition, a section of this series will be concerned with examples of obstacles to learning. All of these specific special needs can be seen on a continuum ranging from mild to severe, or from temporary and transient to long-standing or permanent. These include difficulties in learning or in adjustment and behaviour, as well as problems resulting largely from sensory or physical impairments or from difficulties of communication from whatever cause. We hope that teachers will consult the volumes in this section for guidance on working with children with specific difficulties.

The series aims to make a modest 'distance learning' contribution to meeting the needs of teachers working with the whole range of pupils with special educational needs by offering a set of resource materials relating to specific areas of the primary and secondary curriculum and by suggesting ways in which learning obstacles, whatever their origin, can be identified and addressed.

We hope that these materials will not only be used for private study but be subjected to critical scrutiny by school-based inservice groups sharing common curricular interests and by staff of institutions of higher education concerned with both special needs teaching and specific curriculum areas. The series has been planned to provide a resource for Local Education Authority (LEA) advisers, specialist teachers from all sectors of the education service, educational psychologists, and teacher working parties. We hope that the books will provide a stimulus for dialogue and serve as catalysts for improved practice.

It is our hope that parents will also be encouraged to read about new ideas in teaching children with special needs so that they can be in a better position to work in partnership with teachers on the basis of an informed and critical understanding of current difficulties and developments. The goal of 'Education for All' can only be reached if we succeed in developing a working partnership between teachers, pupils, parents, and the community at large.

ELEMENTS OF A WHOLE-SCHOOL APPROACH

Meeting special educational needs in ordinary schools is much more than a process of opening school doors to admit children previously placed in special schools. It involves a radical re-examination of what all schools have to offer all children. Our efforts will be judged in the long term by our success with children who are already in ordinary schools but whose needs are not being met, for whatever reason.

The additional challenge of achieving full educational as well as social integration for children now in special schools needs to be seen in the wider context of a major reappraisal of what ordinary schools have to offer the pupils already in them. The debate about integration of handicapped and disabled children in ordinary schools should not be allowed to overshadow the movement for curriculum reform in the schools themselves. If successful, this could promote the fuller integration of the children already in the schools.

If this is the aim of current policy, as it is of this series of unit texts, we have to begin by examining ways in which schools and school policies can themselves be a major element in children's difficulties.

Can schools cause special needs?

Traditionally, we have looked for causes of learning difficulty in the child. Children have been subjected to tests and investigations by doctors, psychologists and teachers with the aim of pinpointing the nature of the problem and in the hope that this might lead to specific programmes of teaching and intervention. We less frequently ask ourselves whether what and how we teach and the way in which we organise and manage our schools could themselves be a major cause of children's difficulties.

The shift of emphasis towards a whole-school policy is sometimes described in terms of a move away from the deficit or medical model of special education towards a more environmental or ecological model. Clearly, we are concerned here with an interaction between the two. No one would deny that the origins of some learning difficulties do lie in the child. But even where a clear cause can be established — for example, a child with severe brain damage, or one with a serious sensory or motor disorder — it would be simplistic to attribute all the child's learning difficulties to the basic impairment alone.

The ecological model starts from the position that the growth and development of children can be understood only in relation to the nature of their interactions with the various environments which impinge on them and with which they are constantly interacting. These environments include the home and each individual member of the immediate and extended family. Equally important are other children in the neighbourhood and at school, as well as people with whom the child comes into casual or closer contact. We also need to consider the local and wider community and its various institutions — not least, the powerful influence of television, which for some children represents more hours of information intake than is provided by teachers during eleven years of compulsory education. The ecological model thus describes a gradually widening series of concentric circles, each of which provides a powerful series of influences and possibilities for interaction — and therefore learning.

Schools and schooling are only one of many environmental influences affecting the development and learning of children. A great deal has been learned from other environments before the child enters school and much more will be learned after the child leaves full-time education. Schools represent a relatively powerful series of environments, not all concerned with formal learning. During the hours spent in school, it is hard to estimate the extent to which the number and nature of the interactions experienced by any one child are directly concerned with formal teaching and learning. Social interactions with other children also need to be considered.

Questions concerned with access to the curriculum lie at the heart of any whole-school policy. What factors limit the access of certain children to the curriculum? What modifications are necessary to ensure fuller curriculum access? Are there areas of the curriculum from which some children are excluded? Is this because they are thought 'unlikely to be able to benefit'? And even if they are physically present, are there particular lessons or activities which are inaccessible because textbooks or worksheets demand a level of literacy and comprehension which effectively prevent access? Are there tasks in which children partly or wholly fail to understand the language which the teacher is using? Are some teaching styles inappropriate for individual children?

Is it possible that some learning difficulties arise from the ways in which schools are organised and managed? For example, what messages are we conveying when we separate some children from others? How does the language we use to describe certain children reflect our own values and assumptions? How do schools transmit value judgements about children who succeed and those who do not? In the days when there was talk of comprehensive schools being 'grammar schools for all', what hope was there for children who were experiencing significant learning difficulties? And even today, what messages are we transmitting to children and their peers when we exclude them from participation in some school activities? How many children with special needs will be entered for the new General Certificate of Secondary Education (GCSE) examinations? How many have taken or will take part in Technical and Vocational Education Initiative (TVEI) schemes?

The argument here is not that all children should have access to all aspects of the curriculum. Rather it is a plea for the individualisation of learning opportunities for all children. This requires a broad curriculum with a rich choice of learning opportunities designed to suit the very wide range of individual needs.

Curriculum reform

The last decade has seen an increasingly interventionist approach by Her Majesty's Inspectors of Education (HMI), by officials of the Department of Education and Science (DES) and by individual Secretaries of State. The 'Great Debate', allegedly beginning in 1976, led to a flood of curriculum guidelines from the centre. The garden is secret no longer. Whilst Britain is far from the centrally imposed curriculum found in some other countries, government is increasingly insisting that schools must reflect certain key areas of experience for all pupils, and in particular those concerned with the world of work (*sic*), with science and technology, and with economic awareness. These priorities are also reflected in the prescriptions for teacher education laid down with an increasing degree of firmness from the centre.

There are indications that a major reappraisal of curriculum content and access is already under way and seems to be well supported by teachers. Perhaps the best known and most recent examples can be found in the series of Inner London Education Authority (ILEA) reports concerned with secondary, primary and special education, known as the Hargreaves, Thomas and Fish Reports (ILEA, 1984, 1985a, 1985b). In particular, the Hargreaves Report envisaged a radical reform of the secondary curriculum, based to some extent on his book *Challenge for the Comprehensive School* (Hargreaves, 1982). This envisages a major shift of emphasis from the 'cognitive–academic' curriculum of many secondary schools towards one emphasising more personal involvement by pupils in selecting their own patterns of study from a wider range of choice. If the proposals in these reports were to be even partially implemented, pupils with special needs would stand to benefit from such a wholesale review of the curriculum of the school as a whole.

Pupils with special needs also stand to benefit from other developments in mainstream education. These include new approaches to records of achievement, particularly 'profiling' and a greater emphasis on criterion-referenced assessment. Some caution has already been expressed about the extent to which the new GCSE examinations will reach less able children previously excluded from the Certificate of Secondary Education. Similar caution is justified in relation to the TVEI and the Certificate of Pre-Vocational Education (CPVE). And what about the new training initiatives for school leavers and the 14–19 age group in general? Certainly, the pronouncements of the Manpower Services Commission (MSC) emphasise a policy of provision for all, and have made specific arrangements for young people with special needs, including those with disabilities. In the last analysis, society and its institutions will be judged by their success in preparing the majority of young people to make an effective and valued contribution to the community as a whole.

A CLIMATE OF CHANGE

Despite the very real and sometimes overwhelming difficulties faced by schools and teachers as a result of underfunding and professional unrest, there are encouraging signs of change and reform which, if successful, could have a significant impact not only on children with special needs but on all children. Some of these are briefly mentioned below.

The campaign for equal opportunities

First, we are more aware of the need to confront issues concerned with civil rights and equal opportunities. All professionals concerned with human services are being asked to examine their own attitudes and practices and to question the extent to which these might unwittingly or even deliberately discriminate unfairly against some sections of the population.

We are more conscious than ever of the need to take positive steps to promote the full access of girls and women not only to full educational opportunities but also to the whole range of community resources and services, including employment, leisure, housing, social security and the right to property. We have a similar concern for members of ethnic and religious groups who have been and still are victims of discrimination and restricted opportunities for participation in society and its institutions. It is no accident that the title of the Swann Report on children from ethnic minorities was *Education for All* (Committee of Inquiry, 1985). This too is the theme of the present series and the underlying aim of the movement to meet the whole range of special needs in ordinary schools.

The equal opportunities movement has not itself always fully accepted people with disabilities and special needs. At national level, there is no legislation specifically concerned with discrimination against people with disabilities, though this does exist in some other countries. The Equal Opportunities Commission does not concern itself with disability issues. On the other hand, an increasing number of local authorities and large corporations claim to be 'Equal Opportunities Employers', specifically mentioning disability alongside gender, ethnicity and sexual orientation. Furthermore, the 1986 Disabled Persons Act, arising from a private member's Bill and now on the statute book, seeks to carry forward for adults some of the more positive features of the 1981 Education Act — for example, it provides for the rights of all people with disabilities to take part or be represented in discussion and decision-making concerning services provided for them.

These developments, however, have been largely concerned with children or adults with disabilities, rather than with children already in ordinary schools. Powerful voluntary organisations such as MENCAP (the Royal Society for Mentally Handicapped Children and Adults) and the Spastics Society have helped to raise political and public awareness of the needs of children with disabilities and have fought hard and on the whole successfully to secure better services for them and for their families. Similarly, organisations of adults with disabilities, such as the British Council of Organisations for Disabled People, are pressing hard for better quality, integrated education, given their own personal experiences of segregated provision.

Special needs and social disadvantage

Even these developments have largely bypassed two of the largest groups now in special schools: those with moderate learning difficulties and those with emotional and behavioural difficulties. There are no powerful pressure groups to speak for them, for the same reason that no pressure groups speak for the needs of children with special needs already in ordinary schools. Many of these children come from families which do not readily form themselves into associations and pressure groups. Many of their parents are unemployed, on low incomes or dependent on social security; many live in overcrowded conditions in poor quality housing or have long-standing health problems. Some members of these families have themselves experienced school failure and rejection as children.

Problems of poverty and disadvantage are common in families of children with special needs already in ordinary schools. Low achievement and social disadvantage are clearly associated, though it is important not to assume that there is a simple relation between them. Although most children from socially disadvantaged backgrounds have not been identified as low achieving, there is still a high correlation between social-class membership and educational achievement, with middle-class children distancing themselves increasingly in educational achievements and perhaps also socially from children from working-class backgrounds — another form of segregation within what purports to be the mainstream.

The probability of socially disadvantaged children being identified as having special needs is very much greater than in other children. An early estimate suggested that it was more than seven times as high, when social disadvantage was defined by the presence of all three of the following indices: overcrowding (more than 1.5 persons per room), low income (supplementary benefit or free school meals) and adverse family circumstances (coming from a single-parent home or a home with more than five children) (Wedge and Prosser, 1973). Since this study was published, the number of families coming into these categories has greatly increased as a result of deteriorating economic conditions and changing social circumstances.

In this wider sense, the problem of special needs is largely a problem of social disadvantage and poverty. Children with special needs are therefore doubly vulnerable to underestimation of their abilities: first, because of their family and social backgrounds, and second, because of their low achievements. A recent large-scale study of special needs provision in junior schools suggests that while teachers' attitudes to low-achieving children are broadly positive, they are pessimistic about the ability of such children to derive much benefit from increased special needs provision (Croll and Moses, 1985).

Partnership with parents

The Croll and Moses survey of junior school practice confirms that teachers still tend to attribute many children's difficulties to adverse home circumstances. How many times have we heard comments along the lines of 'What can you expect from a child from that kind of family?' Is this not a form of stereotyping at least as damaging as racist and sexist attitudes?

Partnership with parents of socially disadvantaged children thus presents a very different challenge from that portrayed in the many reports of successful practice in some special schools. Nevertheless, the challenge can be and is being met. Paul Widlake's recent books (1984, 1985) give the lie to the oft-expressed view that some parents are 'not interested in their child's education'. Widlake documents project after project in which teachers and parents have worked well together. Many of these projects have involved teachers visiting homes rather than parents attending school meetings. There is also now ample research to show that children whose parents listen to them reading at home tend to read better and to enjoy reading more than other children (Topping and Wolfendale, 1985; see also Sheila Wolfendale's *Primary Schools and Special Needs*, in the present series).

Support in the classroom

If teachers in ordinary schools are to identify and meet the whole range of special needs, including those of children currently in special schools, they are entitled to support. Above all, this must come from the head teacher and from the senior staff of the school; from any special needs specialists or teams already in the school; from members of the new advisory and support services, as well as from educational psychologists, social workers and any health professionals who may be involved.

This support can take many forms. In the past, support meant removing the child for considerable periods of time into the care of remedial teachers either within the school or coming from outside. Withdrawal now tends to be discouraged, partly because it is thought to be another form of segregation within the ordinary school, and therefore in danger of isolating and stigmatising children, and partly because it deprives children of access to lessons and activities available to other children. In a major survey of special needs provision in middle and secondary schools, Clunies-Ross and Wimhurst (1983) showed that children with special needs were most often withdrawn from science and modern languages in order to find the time to give them extra help with literacy.

Many schools and LEAs are exploring ways in which both teachers and children can be supported without withdrawing children from ordinary classes. For example, special needs teachers increasingly are working alongside their colleagues in ordinary classrooms, not just with a small group of children with special needs but also with all children. Others are working as consultants to their colleagues in discussing the level of difficulty demanded of children following a particular course or specific lesson. An account of recent developments in consultancy is given in Hanko (1985), with particular reference to children with difficulties of behaviour or adjustment.

Although traditional remedial education is undergoing radical reform, major problems remain. Implementation of new approaches is uneven both between and within LEAs. Many schools still have a remedial department or are visited by peripatetic remedial teachers who withdraw children for extra tuition in reading with little time for consultation with school staff. Withdrawal is still the preferred mode of providing extra help in primary schools, as suggested in surveys of current practice (Clunies-Ross and Wimhurst, 1983; Hodgson, Clunies-Ross and Hegarty, 1984; Croll and Moses, 1985).

Nevertheless, an increasing number of schools now see withdrawal as only one of a widening range of options, only to be used where the child's individually assessed needs suggest that this is indeed the most appropriate form of provision. Other alternatives are now being considered. The overall aim of most of these involves the development of a working partnership between the ordinary class teacher and members of teams with particular responsibility for meeting special needs. This partnership can take a variety of forms, depending on particular circumstances and individual preferences. Much depends on the sheer credibility of special needs teachers, their perceived capacity to offer support and advice and, where necessary, direct, practical help.

We can think of the presence of the specialist teacher as being on a continuum of visibility. A 'high-profile' specialist may sit alongside a pupil with special needs, providing direct assistance and support in participating in activities being followed by the rest of the class. A 'low-profile' specialist may join with a colleague in what is in effect a team-teaching situation, perhaps spending a little more time with individuals or groups with special needs. An even lower profile is provided by teachers who may not set foot in the classroom at all but who may spend considerable periods of time in discussion with colleagues on ways in which the curriculum can be made more accessible to all children in the class, including the least able. Such discussions may involve an examination of textbooks and other reading assignments for readability, conceptual difficulty and relevance of content, as well as issues concerned with the presentation of the material, language modes and complexity used to explain what is required, and the use of different approaches to teacher–pupil dialogue.

IMPLICATIONS FOR TEACHER TRAINING

Issues of training are raised by the authors of the three overview works in this series but permeate all the volumes concerned with specific areas of the curriculum or specific areas of special needs.

The scale and complexity of changes taking place in the field of special needs and the necessary transformation of the teacher-training curriculum imply an agenda for teacher training that is nothing less than retraining and supporting every teacher in the country in working with pupils with special needs.

Although teacher training represented one of the three major priorities identified by the Warnock Committee, the resources devoted to this priority have been meagre, despite a strong commitment to training from teachers, LEAs, staff of higher education, HMI and the DES itself. Nevertheless, some positive developments can be noted (for more detailed accounts of developments in teacher education see Sayer and Jones, 1985 and Robson, Sebba, Mittler and Davies, 1988).

Initial training

At the initial training level, we now find an insistence that all teachers in training must be exposed to a compulsory component concerned with meeting special needs in the ordinary school. The Council for the Accreditation of Teacher Education (CATE) and HMI seem set to enforce these criteria; institutions that do not meet them will not be accredited for teacher training.

Although this policy is welcome from a special needs perspective, many questions remain. Where will the staff to teach these courses come from? What happened to the Warnock recommendations for each teacher-training institution to have a small team of staff specifically concerned with this area? Even when a team exists, they can succeed in 'permeating' a special needs element into initial teacher training only to the extent that they influence all their fellow specialist tutors to widen their teaching perspectives to include children with special needs.

Special needs departments in higher education face similar problems to those confronting special needs teams in secondary schools. They need to gain access to and influence the work of the whole institution. They also need to avoid the situation where the very existence of an active special needs department results in colleagues regarding special needs as someone else's responsibility, not theirs.

Despite these problems, the outlook in the long term is favourable. More and more teachers in training are at least receiving an introduction to special needs; are being encouraged to seek out information on special needs policy and practice in the schools in which they are doing their teaching practice, and are being introduced to a variety of approaches to meeting their needs. Teaching materials are being prepared specifically for initial teacher-training students. Teacher trainers have also been greatly encouraged by the obvious interest and commitment of students to children with special needs; optional and elective courses on this subject have always been over-subscribed.

Inservice courses for designated teachers

Since 1983, the government has funded a series of one-term full-time courses in polytechnics and universities to provide intensive training for designated teachers with specific responsibility for pupils with special needs in ordinary schools (see *Meeting Special Needs in Ordinary Schools* by Seamus Hegarty in this series for information on research on evaluation of their effectiveness). These courses are innovative in a number of respects. They bring LEA and higher-education staff together in a productive working partnership. The seconded teacher, headteacher, LEA adviser and higher-education tutor enter into a commitment to train and support the teachers in becoming change agents in their own schools. Students spend two days a week in their own schools initiating and implementing change. All teachers with designated responsibilities for pupils with special needs have the right to be considered for these one-term courses, which are now a national priority area for which central funding is available. However, not all teachers can gain access to these courses as the institutions are geographically very unevenly distributed.

Other inservice courses

The future of inservice education for teachers (INSET) in education in general and special needs in particular is in a state of transition. Since April 1987, the government has abolished the central pooling arrangements which previously funded courses and has replaced these by a system in which LEAs are required to identify their training requirements and to submit these to the DES for funding. LEAs are being asked to negotiate training needs with each school as part of a policy of staff development and appraisal. Special needs is one of nineteen national priority areas that will receive 70 per cent funding from the DES, as is training for further education (FE) staff with special needs responsibilities.

These new arrangements, known as Grant Related Inservice Training (GRIST), will change the face of inservice training for all teachers but time is needed to assess their impact on training opportunities and teacher effectiveness (see Mittler, 1986, for an interim account of the implications of the proposed changes). In the meantime, there is serious concern about the future of secondments for courses longer than one term. Additional staffing will also be needed in higher education to respond to the wider range of demand.

An increasing number of 'teaching packages' have become available for teachers working with pupils with special needs. Some (though not all) of these are well designed and evaluated. Most of them are school-based and can be used by small groups of teachers working under the supervision of a trained tutor.

The best known of these is the Special Needs Action Programme (SNAP) originally developed for Coventry primary schools (Muncey and Ainscow, 1982) but now being adapted for secondary schools. This is based on a form of pyramid training in which co-ordinators from each school are trained to train colleagues in their own school or sometimes in a consortium of local schools. Evaluation by a National Foundation for Educational Research (NFER) research team suggests that SNAP is potentially an effective approach to school-based inservice training, providing that strong management support is guaranteed by the headteacher and by senior LEA staff (see Hegarty, *Meeting Special Needs in Ordinary Schools*, this series, for a brief summary).

Does training work?

Many readers of this series of books are likely to have recent experience of training courses. How many of them led to changes in classroom practice? How often have teachers been frustrated by their inability to introduce and implement change in their schools on returning from a course? How many heads actively support their staff in becoming change agents? How many teachers returning from advanced one-year courses have experienced 'the re-entry phenomenon'? At worst, this is quite simply being ignored: neither the LEA adviser, nor the head nor any one else asks about special interests and skills developed on the course and how these could be most effectively put to good use in the school. Instead, the returning member of staff is put through various re-initiation rituals ('Enjoyed your holiday?'), or is given responsibilities bearing no relation to interests developed on the course. Not infrequently, colleagues with less experience and fewer qualifications are promoted over their heads during their absence.

At a time of major initiatives in training, it may seem churlish to raise questions about the effectiveness of staff training. It is necessary to do so because training resources are limited and because the morale and motivation of the teaching force depend on satisfaction with what is offered — indeed, on opportunities to negotiate what is available with course providers. Blind faith in training for training's sake soon leads to disillusionment and frustration.

For the last three years, a team of researchers at Manchester University and Huddersfield Polytechnic have been involved in a DES funded project which aimed to assess the impact of a range of inservice courses on teachers working with pupils with special educational needs (see Robson, Sebba, Mittler and Davies, 1988, for a full account and Sebba and Robson, 1987, for a briefer interim report). A variety of courses was evaluated; some were held for one evening a week for a term; others were one-week full time; some were award-bearing, others were not. The former included the North-West regional diploma in special needs, the first example of a course developed in total partnership between a university and a polytechnic which allows students to take modules from either institution and also gives credit recognition to specific Open University and LEA courses. The research also evaluated the effectiveness of an already published and disseminated course on behavioural methods of teaching — the EDY course (Farrell, 1985).

Whether or not the readers of these books are or will be experiencing a training course, or whether their training consists only of the reading of one or more of the books in this series, it may be useful to conclude by highlighting a number of challenges facing teachers and teacher trainers in the coming decades.

1.   We are all out of date in relation to the challenges that we face in our work.

2. Training in isolation achieves very little. Training must be seen as part of a wider programme of change and development of the institution as a whole.

3. Each LEA, each school and each agency needs to develop a strategic approach to staff development, involving detailed identification of training and development needs with the staff as a whole and with each individual member of staff.

4. There must be a commitment by management to enable the staff member to try to implement ideas and methods learned on the course.

5. This implies a corresponding commitment by the training institutions to prepare the student to become an agent of change.

6. There is more to training than attending courses. Much can be learned simply by visiting other schools, seeing teachers and other professionals at work in different settings and exchanging ideas and experiences. Many valuable training experiences can be arranged within a single school or agency, or by a group of teachers from different schools meeting regularly to carry out an agreed task.

7. There is now no shortage of books, periodicals, videos and audio-visual aids concerned with the field of special needs. Every school should therefore have a small staff library which can be used as a resource by staff and parents. We hope that the present series of unit texts will make a useful contribution to such a library.

The publishers and I would like to thank the many people – too numerous to mention — who have helped to create this series. In particular we would like to thank the Associate Editors, James Hogg, Peter Pumfrey, Tessa Roberts and Colin Robson, for their active advice and guidance; the Honorary Advisory Board, Neville Bennett, Marion Blythman, George Cooke, John Fish, Ken Jones, Sylvia Phillips, Klaus Wedell and Phillip Williams, for their comments and suggestions; and the teachers, teacher trainers and special needs advisers who took part in our information surveys.

We would particularly like to thank John Fitzpatrick for his assistance during the production of *Encouraging Expression*.

Professor Peter Mittler
University of Manchester

REFERENCES

Clunies-Ross, L. and Wimhurst, S. (1983) *The Right Balance: Provision for Slow Learners in Secondary Schools*. Windsor: NFER/Nelson.

Committee of Inquiry (1985) *Education for All*. London: HMSO (The Swann Report).

Croll, P. and Moses, D. (1985) *One in Five: The Assessment and Incidence of Special Educational Needs*. London: Routledge & Kegan Paul.

Farrell, P. (ed.) (1985) *EDY: Its Impact on Staff Training in Mental Handicap*. Manchester: Manchester University Press.

Hanko, G. (1985) *Special Needs in Ordinary Classrooms: An Approach to Teacher Support and Pupil Care in Primary and Secondary Schools*. Oxford: Blackwell.

Hargreaves, D. (1982) *Challenge for the Comprehensive School*. London: Routledge & Kegan Paul.

Hodgson, A., Clunies-Ross, L. and Hegarty, S. (1984) *Learning Together*. Windsor: NFER/Nelson.

Inner London Education Authority (1984) *Improving Secondary Education*. London: ILEA (The Hargreaves Report).

Inner London Education Authority (1985a) *Improving Primary Schools*. London: ILEA (The Thomas Report).

Inner London Education Authority (1985b) *Equal Opportunities for All?* London: ILEA (The Fish Report).

Mittler, P. (1986) The new look in inservice training, *British Journal of Special Education*, **13**, 50–51.

Muncey, J. and Ainscow, M. (1982) Launching SNAP in Coventry. *Special Education: Forward Trends*, **10**, 3–5.

Robson, C., Sebba, J., Mittler, P. and Davies, G. (1988) *Inservice Training and Special Needs: Running Short School-Focused Courses*. Manchester: Manchester University Press.

Sayer, J. and Jones, N. (eds) (1985) *Teacher Training and Special Educational Needs*. Beckenham: Croom Helm.

Sebba, J. and Robson, C. (1987) The development of short, school-focused INSET courses in special educational needs. *Research Papers in Education* **2**, 1–29.

Topping, K. and Wolfendale, S. (eds) (1985) *Parental Involvement in Children's Reading*. Beckenham: Croom Helm.

Wedge, P. and Prosser, H. (1973) *Born to Fail?* London: National Children's Bureau.

Widlake, P. (1984) *How to Reach the Hard to Teach*. Milton Keynes: Open University Press.

Widlake, P. (1985) *Reducing Educational Disadvantage*. London: Routledge & Kegan Paul.

—1—

Introduction

This book is about art and craft, drama, music, literature, dance and physical education for children with special educational needs in primary schools. These subjects will be referred to generally as aesthetic subjects or the arts. It is hoped that readers will agree to accept them for practical purposes as a group with a shared emphasis on expression, creation and appreciation and to suspend their awareness of differences in order to focus on what they have in common.

The first problem with a book of this kind is one of definition. In the proposal to discuss areas of the curriculum that provide children with the opportunity to be creative, to express themselves and to develop appreciation, there could be detected a suggestion that other areas of the curriculum do not do this; that it is not possible to be creative in mathematics, to express oneself through a study of the environment or to reach an appreciation of order through scientific observation. No such implication is intended. Such activities are an essential part of learning in any curriculum area if children are truly to assimilate and be able to use what they learn. The writers of other books in the series have stressed this.

The purpose of this book, however, is to examine those areas that draw most essentially on the human propensity to create, to express and to appreciate. These are the kind of experiences offered by the arts and they are regarded as so vital to the development of the child that it is considered legitimate to isolate them and devote a complete book to their exploration.

A curriculum that neglects opportunities for creation, expression and appreciation would be a sterile curriculum indeed. This would be true for any children but it is particularly so for children whose special needs may render the liberating and enriching effects of experiences in the arts more necessary, or make success in other areas of the curriculum more difficult to achieve.

What special contributions might we expect the arts to make to children's development? The Assessment of Performance Unit (APU) (1983) statement on aesthetic development suggests that involvement with the arts can 'extend and deepen the capacity to learn about oneself' (p. 3) and also increase perceptiveness and insight about life and the world around us. A view of just how these essential benefits might occur is presented in the report of an enquiry into the arts in school sponsored by the Gulbenkian Foundation (Gulbenkian, 1982). Six important areas in which the arts might contribute to children's education are identified as:

(a)   ... developing the full variety of human intelligence;
(b)   ... developing the capacity for creative thought and action;
(c)   ... the education of feeling and sensibility;
(d)   ... the exploration of values;
(e)   ... understanding cultural change and differences; and
(f)   ... developing physical and perceptual skills. (pp. 10–12)

The Gulbenkian propositions are more specific and would indeed lead to the general development of self-knowledge and sensitive awareness of the world proposed by the APU, but they go further in that there is a suggestion that the arts can also extend the capacity to learn. The arts, according to the Gulbenkian Committee, 'are fundamental ways of organising our understanding of the world' (p. 10). As such they are essential to the development of the full range of children's intelligence and abilities.

Experience with the arts can be seen then as a major means of personal and intellectual development. The arts provide alternative means of expression and bestow a sense of the worth both of self and others. Such experience is likely to be of the utmost value to all children, but to none more than those with special educational needs. For children with learning difficulties, whether these arise from intellectual immaturity, specific disability or general disadvantaging circumstances, it is essential to search for and take advantage of any way into learning, and to ensure that they have the chance to become skilful in areas other than the conventionally academic. For children with difficulties in communication, whether these arise from physical or social problems, every opportunity for alternative means of expression is important. Children with emotional or behavioural problems, who are frequently subject to frustration and stress, may derive particular benefit from opportunities to create and to explore their own feelings. Also, as Brennan (1985) points out, the problem with emotionally disturbed children often lies in the limited nature of their perceptions of others; experience with the arts may be one of the most effective ways of increasing awareness in this area.

Almost all children with special needs face difficulties in forming adequate concepts of self. Occasionally the difficulty may lie in an unrealistically high assessment of self. Much more frequently the problem is the reverse. Children with special needs are more likely to be despondent about themselves and to develop a poor self-image in relation to other children. Involvement in expressive and creative work can provide an alternative opportunity to excel and hence to put a higher value on their own achievements and arrive at a greater sense of their own worth.

In view of the prospect of such positive outcomes from experiences in the aesthetic areas of the curriculum, it is not surprising that there is considerable official support for providing them for all children, including those with special needs, at all age levels in the educational system. A series of official publications has emphasised the importance of involvement in the arts and the influential DES paper *The Curriculum from 5 to 16* (1985) includes the *aesthetic and creative* among the nine areas considered to be essential in the curriculum of all schools. It is admittedly a little disturbing that the *National Curriculum Consultation Document* (July 1987) suggests that the majority of curriculum time at primary level should be devoted to core subjects and makes little mention of the arts in relation to primary schools, but this may be due to the fact that government thinking about the primary curriculum appears to be as yet undeveloped compared with that on the secondary curriculum. Certainly, there can be no doubt of the seriousness with which experience in the arts is regarded by HMI in the field.

Unfortunately, an official blessing is no guarantee of performance. The reality of the situation appears to be that education in the arts is much neglected in schools. A succession of studies and surveys (e.g. Barker Lunn, 1984; Bennett et al., 1984; DES, 1978 and 1982) has found that primary schools tend to concentrate on basic skills and to give a low priority to distinctively expressive or creative work. The image of the progressive primary school, alive with children creating things and exploring a variety of means of expression, appears somewhat illusory. If anything, progression would seem to lie in a retreat from the Plowden ideal. As Gammage (1986) gloomily observes, after reviewing a considerable number of studies, they 'show primary curriculum content and style to be something easily recognizable to past generations' (p. 65).

The Gulbenkian Committee (1982) fear an actual decline in the status of the arts in education as pressure on resources increases and an emphasis on market forces favours the utilitarian. There is some danger, they consider, of the arts being perceived as pleasurable and good for leisure times, but inessential, in terms of the real business of educating children for the world of work. Abbs (1987) sees a current prospect of the arts being set so far from the core of a national curriculum that many children may experience little or no involvement. He considers that it is impossible to exaggerate the plight of the arts in schools.

The preoccupation with basic skills is not confined to the mainstream primary system. It was a tendency observed in special schools by the Schools Council team (Wilson, 1981). Indeed, there has long been a particular tendency in special education to concentrate on what are considered the more essential parts of the curriculum at the expense of other experiences. The very terminology used by Tansley and Gulliford (1960), for example, to promote their *core* and *periphery* approach to work with slow learners consigned aesthetic activities to a minor rôle. Even Brennan (1985) appears less than wholehearted in his support of expressive and creative activities: he suggests pushing art and craft and physical education out of the classroom of the boarding school in order to clear 'precious schoolroom time for other curriculum activities' (p. 124).

As Alexander (1984) observes, one has only to look at the relative impact made by the Cockcroft and Gulbenkian Reports to gain an insight into the perceived importance of such a subject as mathematics, considered essential to the curriculum, compared with the arts, which are considered to be only a pleasant frill to the curriculum. Most teachers would regard it as professionally important at least to know what the Cockcroft Report is about, whereas many are likely never to have heard of the Gulbenkian Report.

It is not difficult to see why the arts do not receive a high priority in most schools. Teachers are understandably concerned that children should reach an adequate standard of basic skills that will stand them in good stead in life beyond school. The more difficulty children have in acquiring basic skills, the more concerned their teachers become. We cannot be by any means sure that simply spending more time on the same thing will lead to greater achievement though. On the contrary, according to HMI (1978) in their survey of primary education in England, there was no evidence 'that a narrower curriculum enabled children to do better in the basic skills' (p. 114).

Many teachers may feel unsure about their ability to teach the arts well. The recent NFER survey (Cleave and Sharp, 1987) showed that teachers may well lack confidence as a result of inadequate training in these areas of the curriculum, for courses of initial preparation for teaching were found to be far from consistent in their coverage of the arts.

There is undeniably some difficulty in organising teaching of the arts. In terms of planning, it is considerably easier to draw up a list of well-defined objectives in the cognitive dimension of human experience and then to set about achieving these than it is to pin down the affective domain with which expressive and creative arts are particularly concerned. It resists neat categorisation and as Kelly (1986) notes 'this aspect of human experience continues to run through the fingers of all who try to capture it in this way' (p. 193). In terms of putting planning into practice, any activity that encourages children to create and to express themselves tends to require meticulous yet open-ended preparation. It also runs the risk of being messy and troublesome to clear away and threatens constantly to get out of hand. With children who need a high level of support or present particular behavioural problems, teaching the arts is likely to be specially demanding. It is understandable that many teachers are daunted by the prospect. Work in basic skills, which tends to keep children sitting still and with which there is an easily definable goal, can be seen to offer many attractions.

Yet to confine children's classroom activities to basic and largely cognitive skills is to leave large areas of human experience to lie undeveloped or to develop outside school. This is unacceptable to any teacher concerned with the whole child and is particularly so for teachers working with children who have special needs. The teacher of children with special needs cannot afford to neglect promising lines of development. Teaching is a constant search for potential and this can scarcely be conducted adequately if such an important aspect of the child is left unexplored.

Undeniably there are some special problems in teaching the arts with children with special needs, but few that cannot be overcome. There will be difficulties in dance for children with mobility problems, for example, but they can and do dance. Those with visual handicap will be limited in their appreciation of certain forms of art and those with hearing impairment will not be able to share as fully in music experience as others, but they can and do take part, given sensitive teaching. Even these extreme examples of checks on participation in the arts are not insurmountable – as those writing about the various areas will make clear. There are ways of making all areas of the arts in some measure accessible to almost all children, however special their needs. For the majority of children, the aesthetic areas of education present no particular difficulties, and for a small minority the difficulties are not insuperable. Indeed, the most difficult handicap for children with special needs to overcome may be underexpectation on the part of their teachers. The pupils of a teacher who believes participation in any of the arts to be beyond their reach will for the most part prove him or her right. Those pupils fortunate enough to have teachers who believe them capable of involvement in the arts will extend their reach to fulfil their teacher's expectations.

It could be argued that in some respects learning through the arts has distinct advantages. Children can approach the subjects without preliminary skills and can begin to build their sensitivity and their skilfulness in the course of actual participation. It could be argued that experience-based learning occurs more easily and more naturally in the arts than in any other areas of education. For some children, the arts may in fact be the way into other areas of the curriculum since they can provide starting points that are so much more accessible and momentum that can carry children along pathways of exploration that might otherwise elude them.

Indeed, it is difficult to conceive of other areas of the curriculum that have such a potential for contributing to the development of children with special needs. It is sad that the evidence suggests they are frequently denied anything but the most rudimentary experience in the arts. It is not just that the children themselves are denied important opportunities for personal and intellectual development; it is also that we are denied the rich outcomes of creation and performance that may ensue. As Jean Turnbull reminds us, Itzhak Perlman and Stevie Wonder were both children with special needs: had they been denied the opportunity to develop their musical ability we would have been denied the pleasure of listening to their music.

This book consists of five pieces of strong writing that focus on different aspects of the arts. The writers convey both the zeal of the enthusiast and the practical concerns of the teacher. Each chapter is steeped in the personal experience of the writer, yet each is different, for the contributors are, as might be expected, very different people who write in distinctive styles. The exuberance of Dorothy Heathcote writing about drama; the practical determination of Keith Chantry to promote art and craft; the clear and business-like approach of Patricia Sanderson to physical education and dance; the thoughtful sensitivity of John Fitzpatrick writing about literature; and the quiet, informative style of Jean Turnbull exploring the possibilities of music, all contrast with each other. What they all share is a common insistence that their subjects are of special value to children with special needs and a determination to ensure that these subjects are made accessible to all children.

All the writers convey an unbounded enthusiasm and are persuasive in their arguments for including their subject areas in the curriculum of the primary school, outlining the benefits for all children. They are also aware of the danger that the arts may, unfortunately, be most vulnerable to neglect, again for all children but particularly for those with special needs. Keith Chantry and Dorothy Heathcote both complain of the tendency for their subjects not to be treated seriously in schools, to be considered non-academic and therefore, by implication, non-essential. This is one of the first hurdles to be overcome by a teacher of the arts. Even if arts teaching is alive and well in a primary school, however, there is still the danger that children with special needs may be to some degree excluded. This may be because there is a tendency for learning difficulties in other areas to be generalised so that children with reading difficulties, for example, may be considered likely to have difficulties in art and craft and therefore be given simple repetitive tasks. Keith Chantry shows how needlessly restricting this can be. Or it may be particular disabilities make access difficult in some areas and therefore place special demands on a teacher who contemplates involving children with special needs. Jean Turnbull and Patricia Sanderson give good advice and show how easily overcome such difficulties are in the fields of music and physical education and dance.

Far from dwelling on impediments to involving children with special needs in the arts, the writers in this book see the arts as offering to all children the opportunity to take part on equal terms because the arts draw upon and present fundamental human experience. John Fitzpatrick shows how literature emphasises and illuminates the commonality of human experience; personal involvement is open to all children. Dorothy Heathcote's child in a wheelchair is more essentially a cleaner than a child with special needs once she dons a headscarf and begins to participate in the *as if* world of drama. Once it is accepted that children with special needs can take part in the arts on equal terms, however, it is important that they should be accorded equal respect. As Keith Chantry observes, they must be paid the compliment of critical guidance and not just left to experiment, explore or perform without feedback.

The writers are concerned to emphasise the distinctive contribution that the arts can make in providing access to other areas of the curriculum and in promoting children's understanding of other worlds. Dorothy Heathcote, for example, shows in particularly helpful detail how drama can prove to be a vehicle for the study of science, history, art and design and so on, among children who might otherwise find it difficult to get into such subjects. Jean Turnbull describes the skills and concepts acquired through music that can be put to use in other subjects. Patricia Sanderson points to the reciprocal nature of the relationship between the arts and other areas of the curriculum. While scientific principles can be drawn from children's experience of movement, it is also the case that ideas from science can provide many fruitful starting points for dance. John Fitzpatrick describes the entry into other worlds made possible by literature, an experience particularly valuable to children with special needs whose own world may be so tightly circumscribed.

Just as important as the relationship to other areas of the curriculum may be the contribution that the arts may make to children's confidence and sense of worth, personal areas that are often damaged in children with special needs. Patricia Sanderson alerts us to the possibility of children with learning difficulties in other areas of the curriculum excelling in PE or dance, for example, and thereby acquiring status in the eyes of other children. Jean Turnbull shows how music-making is possible for all children and can lead to greatly enhanced self-esteem in children who may be restricted in other means of expressing themselves. Music is a form of communication and therefore of special worth to children for whom communication is difficult.

All the writers also emphasise the intrinsic worth of experience in the arts. For most children, they provide pleasurable experiences that are likely to prove satisfying. More than this, however, the arts offer a distinctive way of experiencing the world. John Fitzpatrick refers to Rosenblatt's description of literature as a 'seeing for yourself, a living through not simply knowledge about'. The experiences of creating, expressing and appreciating that are central to the arts can provide a kind of release, fulfilment, satisfaction and heightened understanding that it may be difficult for children, especially those with varying kinds of learning disability, to obtain through other areas of primary school experience.

There is a great deal of practical advice for teachers who undertake teaching of the arts with children with special needs. Always, the concern is for the particular situation of children for whom learning may be difficult, but of course much of the advice is relevant to the teaching of all children. It is very seldom that a good teaching idea is good only for a small group of children and even if it were conceived as such, teachers, in their constant search for more effective ways of teaching, would find ways of adapting and generalising it. Similarly the positive personal qualities that the writers, again and again, look for from teachers of children with special needs are the kind of personal qualities all children deserve to meet in their teachers. The major difference is likely to be that other children may be less dependent on the excellence of their teachers or the appropriateness of approaches than children with special needs. They may have more defences, more resilience, be better able to cope with shortcomings. For most children with special needs, the attitudes and skilfulness of their teachers and the potential productiveness of learning situations are likely to be of paramount importance.

Without exception, the writers emphasise the need for sensitivity in teachers. Teachers must be alert to difficulties that children may experience in participating in the arts, but determined in their search for ways of overcoming these. They must be enthusiastic for their own subject but sufficiently flexible to allow children to participate in many different ways and at many different levels. They must be imaginative in their constant search for ways to motivate and involve children with special needs.

How is this sensitivity put into practice, for unless it is, nobody benefits? Keith Chantry reminds us of the importance of a business-like approach in teachers, who must understand the subject and know what they are doing. In art and craft, there must be analysis of the situation and forward planning to take account of this; just as in other areas of the curriculum, the arts are not an occasion for woolly thinking. Dorothy Heathcote, too, shows that however strong the element of improvisation may appear to be, good drama depends on planning every step of the way. At times, Patricia Sanderson suggests, it may be helpful to set narrow, clearly defined goals that children understand and are capable of achieving, and which are thus the occasion for success and a consequent enhancement of their self image. Keith Chantry and Patricia Sanderson are both particularly keen to emphasise the importance of good planning and organisation at a practical level, ensuring, for example, that equipment is appropriate and available and that there is a fundamental structure to lessons that children can appreciate. Children must understand what is expected of them, and in this respect the teacher's clarity of explanation is an essential factor. Yet there is always a danger that clear sighted planning may acquire a life of its own and leave no room for error. Keith Chantry reminds us of the importance of risk-taking in creative expression; planning must not be so tight that initiative and creativity in children is stifled and scope for individual response limited.

It is also important to help children to reflect upon and understand their experiences, however, and here the opportunity to discuss seems to be an essential factor. Discussions can help children explore their personal response to books, can help them set their drama experiences into perspective, can encourage them to develop ideas about the effectiveness of different forms of artistic representation. These are difficult ideas to crystallise and all children, but particularly those with special needs, are entitled to the help that can arise from talking together.

The material used with children with special needs must be selected carefully. Jean Turnbull suggests a variety of music suitable for particular situations; John Fitzpatrick recommends stories and poetry that seem to address themselves very directly to the case of children with disabilities of one kind and another, but he reminds us that we must be wary of searching for materials that are too exclusively tailored to special needs. The ultimate criterion must be the capacity of the writing to communicate something of value. All children have more that is common to them than is exceptional, and material of high quality will communicate at that level of commonality. Similarly, Dorothy Heathcote shows how drama themes arise from common situations and can accommodate all children without difficulty.

Yet there are situations where special provision is undoubtedly necessary. In particular, learning for those children with physical or sensory disabilities may depend largely on a teacher's willingness or ability to make adaptations. Here, Jean Turnbull offers useful advice, particularly about singing and the playing of musical instruments. Patricia Sanderson provides helpful guidance on all kinds of physical activity for children with these types of disabilities and shows how there are many ways of developing the physical dimension of their experience, so long as the teacher is sufficiently knowledgeable and prepared to make the kind of provision necessary.

A recurring theme throughout the book is the importance of home support. This is an area where special education has led and ordinary schools have followed; an excellent example of the phenomenon mentioned previously that good ideas seldom remain exclusive but tend to become generalised.

Parents are an important source of information about their children and teachers would be unwise to neglect this when they are attempting to cater for special needs. Help to be gained from parents extends far beyond this, however. If children are enthusiastic, parents are likely to take an interest and help them develop their work outside school; Dorothy Heathcote saw this happening with drama. John Fitzpatrick acknowledges the key rôle that parents are able to play, not only in helping their children become readers but also in promoting the appeal of books. We know that to have support can make a vital difference to children's success in school but, as Patricia Sanderson points out, it is unlikely to be forthcoming unless parents understand the value of the activity concerned. This may be something of a problem with the arts though, where parents' own experience may be somewhat limited, so teachers must always be prepared to explain and justify their subject.

All children deserve to experience the satisfaction of creation, the liberation of expression and the enrichment of appreciation. The aim in this book is to show how children with special needs can be helped to gain access to such experiences for it is no less true of them than it is of other children that 'not to attempt at some stage, and in some form, to involve children in the arts is simply to fail to educate them as fully developed, intelligent and feeling human beings' (Gulbenkian Report, 1982, p. 20).

Tessa Roberts
University of Manchester

REFERENCES

Abbs, P. (1987) *Living Powers: the Arts in Education*. London: Falmer Press.
Alexander, R. J. (1984) *Primary Teaching*. London: Cassell.
APU (1983) *Aesthetic Development*. London: DES.
Barker Lunn, J. (1984) Junior school teachers: their methods and practices. *Educational Research*, **26**, 178–188.
Bennett, N., Desforges, C., Cockburn, A. and Wilkinson, B. (1984) *The Quality of Pupil Learning Experiences*. London: Lawrence Erlbaum.
Brennan, W. K. (1985) *Curriculum for Special Needs*. Milton Keynes: Open University Press.
Cleave, S. and Sharp, C. (1987) *The Arts: a Preparation to Teach*. Slough: NFER.
DES (1978) *Primary Education in England*. London: HMSO.
DES (1982) *Education 5–9*. London: HMSO.
DES (1985) *The Curriculum from 5 to 16*. London: HMSO.
Gammage, P. (1986) *Primary Education: Structure and Content*. London: Harper and Row.
Gulbenkian Foundation (1982) *The Arts in Schools*. London: Calouste Gulbenkian Foundation.
Kelly, A. V. (1986) *Knowledge and Curriculum Planning*. London: Harper and Row.
Tansley, A. E. and Gulliford, R. (1960) *The Education of Slow Learning Children*. London: Routledge & Kegan Paul.
Wilson, M. D. (1981) *The Curriculum in Special Schools*. London: Longman for the Schools Council.

—2—

Drama

Dorothy Heathcote with *Eileen Bell, Mary Bowmaker, Margaret Chilley, June Gibbon, Sharon Oakes, Maggie Pivars and Margaret Vause*

Our brief is to try to communicate something of the expressive and creative possibilities of drama in the context of children with special needs in ordinary primary schools.

Our offerings arise from a conviction that drama is a superb vehicle for bringing children together in natural ways and benefits everyone involved in the activity, not just children with special needs. In fact it frequently is the case that it is the teacher and the other children who derive most from it, because of the gifts that arrive with the special needs people.

All teachers know the problems of staffing, timetable restrictions, opinion and curriculum restraints that can mass up against our trying out unusual combinations, whether of subjects or people. For the same reason, we shall not define the term *special needs* too closely for every teacher will have images of such pupils, whether they be hearing-impaired, have sight problems or physical or mental handicaps. Their very specialness has often bred alienation if not active banishment from those ordinary experiences that most of us take for granted.

The work cited is that of determined teachers working with little expertise, flying by the seats of our pants, learning as we go, by trial and error. Sometimes groups involved have been taught all in the same building, as with Eileen's hearing-impaired unit integrated into a primary school. Sometimes, as with Maggie's physically handicapped class, it has taken superhuman efforts of moving from one site to another and wrestling with timetables before groups could be taught together. Sometimes the children with special needs and the other children have been in one class from the very start because their school believes in mixed-ability teaching anyway. In Margaret's class you meet the high flyers and those having extra help with reading or speech therapy, all learning together most of the time. June teaches children with reading difficulties in two schools on a peripatetic basis and manages to bring her charges into all kinds of encounters with other classes whenever she can. Dorothy does not even have a class but specialises in messing about with other teachers' classes, and bringing in non-teachers to add to the confusion, or adventure, depending on whether you think it is useful or not to do so. They can at this stage speak for themselves about why they go on with this sort of work.

Eileen: I'm a primary teacher and this sort of mixed group teaching is one of the most satisfying things I've ever participated in.

A slow reader in June's class: Well, Miss, in drama you get a second chance.

Sharon: I teach in a community school in the inner city and in drama sessions many less able children work and participate far more confidently than in straight academic teaching.

Maggie, a teacher in a special unit: Drama helps them work together in collaboration, to become engaged in social transactions. Being physically handicapped they find the drama provides a 'feeling real' world in which they can maturely negotiate. Usually the actual world treats them as being much less mature than they really are.

Mary, a music specialist: It's the opportunities for developing social health that I value.

Finally, a 'slow learning' student: This is our best subject because in drama people, even clever ones, listen to you and you're able to really tell people your ideas.

If we now take a stroll into some of their classrooms we can become acquainted with a few of the projects in progress, which will be used to illustrate the theory underpinning this account. In Eileen's classroom some 10-year-old Saxon monks have been working for a term, exploring the meaning of discipline related with work in their scriptorium and the keeping of their religious vows. They have novices beside them who are from the hearing-impaired unit whose teacher has been asking them about monks and what they do and has realised that their ideas of such people are that they are sinister cowled figures bent upon harming their fellow men in shadowy places, usually underground. Whether comics or television are the source of their information we cannot tell, but it is to counter these ideas that our Saxons have taken novices into their scriptorium to share in the work of illuminating parchments, saying their offices and working in the monastic compound. Each monk had selected a way to teach about their life taking into consideration the different hearing difficulties of their novice. Because classroom space is restricted, and monks work in very small cells anyway, it is not possible for the phonic ears and microphones to be used, so the monks have to find forms of teaching that communicate themselves.

You may say, well, what's so special about it? It's only children talking together. But you'd be wrong. That's just what it isn't. There are *no* children here, and *no* child behaviours, for the drama has created an *as if* world of mature perceptions, a framework of considered thought and behaviour, wherein all participants have embraced the yoke of responsibility within this domain of monastic order. The monks are not teaching about *any* monks, but about *our* monastery and why we live as we do. We shall discuss this *as if* factor later.

Maggie's classroom in a special school for physically handicapped pupils has been turned into a five star hotel. Any visitors must instantly set to work, so the mainstream students are hard at work as well. Everyone in the room, including two teachers, staffs and stocks this complex social business using the skills and interests they have. Some type, as normal writing tools are a bit awkward for them. The menus for the day are done, the notices for bedrooms, rules about smoking, valuables and room service, all require accurate statements and appropriate display. Occasionally a mobile worker might assist in pinning something on wall or door when wheelchair-bound people cannot reach. Decisions about routines, jobs, food and service are taken by everyone. The name Sundown Hotel is a consensus choice, after much consideration of the image names can give to a place that offers hospitality.

Two older boys needing extra experience of deep play, but with dignity, are organising the 'select' bar, so they are engaged in filling bottles with water and cake colourings, making labels and designing bottle shapes to be cut out in paper to place behind them on paper drawings of shelves. Many and various are the names for their drinks and spellings are somewhat innovative as yet.

Floor plans have been made to enable cleaning staff and guests, as well as security persons and the manager, to know the way about the many corridors. In spite of the fact that probably no child in the room (and teachers are not allowed to take over with information unless directly requested to do so) has ever visited or stayed in such a place, all seems very reasonable. The classroom has the same space as it always has, but here people move in imaginary space, carried by images in their heads. You pass between a table and a wheelchair and find yourself addressed from within the tea-room. Passing from the table's end, you are in the bar or a bedroom. You know this because you meet the waiter, the housekeeper, the chef or chief barman whose work space is carried in their head and they express their duties through realistic considerations. 'We'll need some more bottles from the cellar, it's going to be a busy night.' 'The menus are ready for the main dining room, please collect them from the secretary.' 'We're short of sheets for floor three.'

The hotel is at present a breeding ground not only for many social experiences but also for much school curriculum work. You have to prepare clear written statements for all kinds of reasons and audiences in a five star hotel. (Have *you* ever had to send a letter to a famous film star indicating that pet snakes are not allowed in public rooms? Well …) Drinks and food have to be priced, stores calculated, laundry priced, accommodation charges worked out for the winter and summer rates, half weeks with or without evening meals or newspapers; it really never stops. You need calculators when it is busy and staff training days for quick adding up, or phoning, or fire practice and especially for tour guides to the Roman Wall and for security advice.

There is one very unusual matter that deserves careful consideration. There are no visible guests. This is 'downstairs' in an 'upstairs, downstairs' world. Oh, there *are* guests, we know about them in our minds and we speak to them on the many telephones from deep within our heads; we complain about them at tea-breaks, and worry over the letters they send us. Their names are in our hotel register, and we make 'photographs' of them in our spare time, how they look to us. Do you see why it is so important that there are no guests? Guests are always coming and going. They need not care that the maid on floor three had a bereavement and came to work just the same; or that the chef has a new Doberman pup because he isn't married and has few friends; or that the barman has a new baby at home.

This concept of working drama breaks a lot of accepted rules. Rules such as: hospital dramas need patients; fairground dramas need the public; circuses need animals; or lawyers in courts need criminals. The only thing that matters is that people begin to care passionately about their work, their standards, their responsibilities. They have enough productive tension in their daily business of coping with their invented families and their huge work loads without having to become worked up about anybody else. Besides, neither monks nor hotel staff need to be bothered with pretending or acting scenes. As a handicapped Maori boy once said in a mental hospital in New Zealand, 'This is true-blue drama, I have it all in my mind. This is the REAL THING, by God.'

Some bizarre ideas can surface, according to the problems people want to deal with. It was a never-to-be-forgotten day when a young Saxon boy escaped from an angry reeve and hid in the monastery and the monks had the terrible problem of facing the reeve's irritable questions and *never told a lie* in spite of his pressing them very hard. Fortunately when he asked directly 'Have you seen the boy?', he did not specify *when* so truthfully they could say that they had 'seen him around the fields'. Narrow shave that! And imagine when a monk, once the excitement was over and the boy, fed and safe for the moment, could say 'You know Mrs Bell, when you were the reeve and you put your hand on the cart where the boy was hiding under the fruit, I thought you'd feel him breathing, and my heart nearly stopped.' The interesting thing here is that 'the boy' was represented on the book trolley by a brown paper cut-out shirt, resting under a tablecloth used to keep the class books clean at night. You cannot put a real boy on a book trolley, but you can agree that a paper shirt, on a book trolley you agree is a fruit cart, represents the danger of discovery and betrayal should you break your vows.

Similarly, when the cleaner in room 301 found a dead body – a beautiful young woman – there was a terrible problem for the staff who had to carry on as usual while being interrogated by plain clothes police, so that the guests should not feel frightened. And what are the correct proceedings for staff, relatives, police? Later on there were ancient bones found behind a thick wall and we had to cope with archaeologists. If it isn't one thing it's another!

Around such work there is a constant flurry of invention, preparation of materials, urgently needed because of the seriousness of the events. All this causes shifts in talk, vocabulary and style of writing. One day might be spent designing new uniforms for staff; another making fingerprint records or planning the hotel swimming pool lighting system. The monastery may need a pectoral cross, new song vellums or some Latin for receiving the new bishop suitably.

June's class have prepared a 'proper script' to perform for some autistic colleagues who are running a fire station. June's class, who need writing experience, have written their script and, because they also need reading experience, are trying it out to see if it fits the situation of a household chip-pan fire. It has not only to sound right but must also look right, or their autistic friends won't know there is a house fire and come quickly and put it out. It might be worth a look at the script if only for the vocabulary when the fire is described, and the accuracy of the telephone call to the fire brigade.

This drama was devised by the children at Broadwood School in the form of a written script illustrated with pictures.

THE CHIP PAN FIRE

Scene: Bert and Peter's house.
Tea time.

BERT: Yes. I'll have some chips. But be careful with the chip pan. Mind it doesn't catch fire.

PETER: I'm always careful Bert.

Peter makes the chips.
Bert reads the newspaper.
The doorbell rings.

BERT: Answer the door.
Peter answers the door.
PETER: Hello there.
VISITOR: I've brought the holiday snaps.
PETER: Come in. I'll make some coffee in a minute.
Bert, Peter and the visitor sit in the settee, looking at the snaps. The
chip pan catches fire. Flames begin to creep out of the pan, over the
cooker, up the curtains, across the floor and out of the door.
The flames crackle, spit, hiss and jump.
PETER: I'll go and make some coffee.
Peter goes towards the kitchen.
PETER: The kitchen's on fire!
VISITOR: Quick! Get the fire brigade!
Bert goes to the telephone.
BERT: Hello. Is that the fire brigade?
There's a fire at number six Woodbeck Road.
I'm Bert Tilsley.
The fire brigade arrive and put out the fire.

So there is a home environment created, a telephone system for
messages and a fire fighting unit, all designed quite specifically to
suit different needs and skill development all in one context.

Dorothy's class, entailing a sighted teacher, a sighted class and a
blind class, are all working at a different kind of experience. The
sighted children needed to empathise with and understand better
how their blind colleagues actually do orientate themselves in their
surroundings. The sighted teacher agreed to take on the rôle of
having had a car accident recently and having been blinded as a
result. He further agreed that he would really wear a mask to shut
out the light all the time the project was running, except when he
was driving to school and would keep a diary of his experiences to
share with the children. Who better than those who had been blind
longer to help his worried sighted friends learn how to help him
adjust? From here on it's all action. Tactile maps are made of his
school so he can find his way to class rooms and up and down stairs.
Sighted children must wear masks and trust themselves to their
blind friends in finding their way round in order to identify with the
problems that their teacher will have. Wearing masks will also help
them understand what the blind children mean when they talk of
using walls and furniture as resonators to know your location in
space; how to hear the ball in a cricket match; how to recognise panic
and disorientation; how to feel another's hands and face in order to
recognise and 'see' people; how to store voices in the memory; how
to make your feet really notice and recall floor sounds and textures;
and how to find your own mouth (for eating), nose (for blowing)

and hair (for combing). At one stage *all* the children and teacher were wearing 'death masks' (we use this term so that you appreciate the image) because the sighted children and the teacher had to be in complete darkness, and the blind children loved the idea of having their eyes covered up too! A case of blind man's bluff?

All the examples have a common motif: the *as if* factor mentioned earlier. Every example has in some way required a complete acceptance of the idea of a fictional situation and/or rôles, even the last one where the teacher had to be treated as if he were newly blind and in desperate circumstances in coping with it. There must never be a muddle about whether the work is real or invented. No confusion about reality and fiction. Because this demarcation is absolutely clear from the start, the *as if* contract is developed into truthfulness. Not true, but filled with truth. Not actual, but virtually truthful, striven-for authenticity. This allows all the participants to sustain the experience so as to engage with outcomes of such events in a reasonable way. If paper bottles can be agreed to become a bar in a five star hotel, then we have a whole domain of endeavours with which we can engage. This is how it works. Paper cut-out bottles labelled by ourselves, some looking full, some nearly empty, breed a host of possibilities. In our case not only a ten-feet thick mediaeval hotel wall behind them, but all the social encounters of interest to us of a posh hotel bar and the behaviours that might be found there. Some of these calm and social, others more desperate, like 'when the wall fell in and they found the old bones'. Any event can be explored provided we trust the *as if* element and the patient development of the will of the class to sustain the possibilities pregnant within any social event, and if we bring to it all the relevant experience we are capable of, in working it out.

The next common motif is the way time works in all dramas. Time functions on two planes. There is the time of the developing events. We might call it chronological for it engages us in sequencing – 'Wait here' says the security guard in the hotel when the dead lady is found in room 301, 'I'll have to get the police.' And we do wait while he telephones, and we know time passes while we watch him busy with the dials on the instrument. We experience it in transit because we have someone to watch, behaving appropriately to our expectations. This is like our real chronological lives. But time is also engaged in a different plane. Because we know that there is actually no dead body in room 301, no chip pan on fire in a house endangering life, we have time to savour, time to perceive and time to reflect upon all such events. This kind of time is not sequential; the Chinese have called it 'great time', chronology-less time. We are in a state of being – knowing, even when we are progressing with the event, how we think it must develop if it is to continue to feel more and more truthful. This is art of course – the perceiving of the doing, the recognising of the forming and shaping. Simultaneously our hotel staff can wait for the police with an exciting shudder up the spine, whilst urging their friend in real life to say such and such, to do this or that. They are in the drama as staff and outside the drama as creators of the events, hot-forging it in these two time dimensions; behaving and reflecting on behaving, both at once. Which enters us now upon a third dimension. Because we take rôles within an event and are not just considering how an event might be, we come into that interesting field of having to hold a legitimate biased view, as we would if the event were real as in life. We enter all real life experiences with a frame of reference through which we make sense of them. These frames are bound to be biased because we bring all our own experience, our prejudices and our current investment to them. Bias is essential to unlocking the power to operate and the will to function in an event. If bias is not built into dramas children have to 'fake' responses out of invention and we have all seen those dramas in classrooms where everything becomes pretended and there is no truth in the behaviour.

In the case of Eileen's monastery, June's chip pan fire and Maggie's hotel, the bias provides the productive tension out of the commitment of the parties to their responsibilities. There is no need for the participants to act or to become 'characters' as actors do in written plays intended for audiences, such as *Julius Caesar*. Cassius is not as Brutus is. Each expresses a unique and special behaviour pattern to bring about their different ends for an audience to ponder on and with which to widen their experience of people. In Maggie's hotel or Eileen's monastery, *because the children are at different levels of ability and comprehension*, it is essential that the skills of the actor are never called for. Instead the important thing is the power to operate at your level of comprehension; to hold honourable power in rôle functioning. Actors playing in *Julius Caesar* subdue personal behaviours in the interest of expressing believable fictional behaviours. In classroom drama the person we really are explores the situation with whatever brain and physical energy and skills we can bring to it. And this power to operate from within fictional situations extends our experience, causes practice of skills, makes us forge talk and understanding 'hot' because we operate from within a bias *as if* we were there.

In this sense Maggie's hotel cleaners who find a body in room 301 are stereotypes of all cleaners. One such, operating from a wheelchair, demands a head scarf, apron and brush 'because all cleaners have to have them'. Thus she gains the expressive power to operate by being recognised as operating from that viewpoint regardless of wheelchair and disability. The headscarf obliterated the wheelchair to all intents and purposes. She did not change to any other kind of person, instead she changed our view of her. This is what productive bias does for us. We express because others agree to our power to operate. Once this is begun, then extension of understanding and in-put of expression and creativity naturally develops. And it does so like ripples in a pool, not like a linear development. Let us call our cleaning lady Joan.

At Level One   in first tentative role of cleaner *Joan knows that cleaners dust, that they wear headscarves.*

At Level Two   in the next encounter as well as the above *Joan knows that they clean in some sort of order or sequence. Room 300 comes before 301. Dusting involves picking things up.*

At Level Three   *Joan knows that cleaners can recognise a dead body when they see one and do something about it.*

At Level Four   *Joan knows that cleaners take notice of things in the room they clean. They can describe things from memory when questioned and because they are cleaners they remember things in a certain way, how they feel when you dust them, how they look – dirty or clean.*

At Level Five   *Joan knows that cleaners can make judgements about the people whose rooms they are cleaning by the evidence they see, even if they have never met the occupants.*

At Level Six   *Joan knows that cleaners work in a hierarchy in a hotel and they had better know the difference between giving opinions about a person and facts about a person, between evidence and conjecture.*

At Level Seven   *Joan knows that cleaners are part of the pattern of the infrastructure of a hotel, just as policemen are part of the pattern of justice and dead bodies are part of the pattern of human behaviour.*

We do not suggest that in the drama Joan works consciously at any of this; it is brought to her realisation when she is ready to perceive it, as the various encounters of hotel life are worked through. She can behave, she can respond, and if now and again she can be helped by the teacher's skill to reflect upon things, then she will occasionally realise what she knows. Most of us do not *own* much of the knowledge we possess and use it in our lives. *To know we know something* is always to feed upon it and extend it in use. This again is a function of art, to be present at moments of perception because we are freed temporarily from the need to meet outcomes in stressful circumstances. This brings us to something we as teachers struggle with all the time; to make the form of the drama contain the possibilities of reflection during the action and not just afterwards.

Some teachers like to 'talk it over afterwards' and of course it can yield reflection. But that reflective device is different from reflection during the action in that there will have been a switch from the right brain thinking, where intuition dominates, to left brain thinking and cognitive recognition. Ideally during creative work both brain functions happen at once if the structure is there for this to take place. An easy example of this is when all Eileen's monks were considering 'What is God's purpose in making man angry?' (remember the reeve?) whilst they are pondering on what to do about the boy, in his presence; or when the hotel staff are collected around the body wondering 'How anyone could have contemplated doing such a thing'. In arts other than drama, such as painting or pottery or sculpture, this reflection naturally happens during the work because the materials for the creation exist outside of us. In dance and drama we *are* the materials, so the brain switch has to be part of the form. This is actually very easy to arrange as we have shown in our example, but there are many more ways to do it.

Many school timetables attest to the notion that drama is a natural tool to use with classes where special needs in pupils can be catered for. This premise is built on a false assumption, or two. It is assumed that drama is non-academic, more intuitive, has no curriculum as you might say, that it is just discovery. This is to a very small degree true. Because it is so flexible (all life is here in the celebration of the affairs of mankind!) it looks a fine idea. The problem is that most of the time in school the need interests of pupils and the curriculum interests of teachers are in conflict and it requires a compromise from both; the teacher has to find a way to create interest and the student must subdue natural need-behaviour. In an academic approach, pupils have to try to become interested through conscious appeal to cognition. If you have a class containing individuals with special needs and of different basic abilities due to such factors as hearing or mobility impairment, the whole affair becomes rife with problems. So in one sense teachers who would use drama methods such as we have shown to put work in context, to provide reasons, albeit artificial and fictional, make even more trouble for themselves. Drama invites the actual behaviour of the participants to emerge as well as providing the opportunity for new behaviours to be explored.

Neither can the teacher in honour resort to the oft-used teacher authority stance. If you are a participant, you can't suddenly pull power, except in situations where either physical or mental hurt may occur to someone. The drama we have been trying out is built upon the assumption that the teacher will not function as either the holder of the best knowledge, or the one who can insist and coerce. Rather we have found that the material and the interests of the pupils eventually become the disciplining factors. 'Stop messing about', says a wine waiter to a chef. We have even found that we can monitor our own behaviours as students and teachers. We did it through filling in a form that started 'I didn't pay attention any of the time, and I distracted others' and ended with 'I kept my drama eyes all the time; I never allowed myself to be distracted; I helped other people to keep their drama eyes.'

So, agreeing that the materials and style of drama is suitable for mixed groups, what can we do to assist the work to matter to all, regardless of what their need interests are? Teachers are quite frightened of unleashing a variety of behaviours in class. Why do we arrange our classes in formal rows so often? Place ourselves at the front? Materials such as we have discussed can cater for a variety of needs, social and academic, but they have to be presented under quite different circumstances, demanding a fair number of skills that, regrettably, are not yet widely taught to teachers, so those who have them are considered charismatic! These skills are high level negotiation skills, which can be mastered if there is a will. We struggle with them all the time for they are subtle in process though easily grasped in theory.

First is the problem, in a culture such as ours where fiction is seen as entertainment, with no use for real life, of winning people to be interested in making a fictional situation. We do not have a village storyteller who is human like ourselves. We have storytellers who are in photographic images, cleverly varied, and associated with a glamour we do not expect to share, except via 'the box'. Almost every public manifestation of fiction is either expensive (been to the pictures with your family lately?) or looks glamorous, as in advertising, or demands an effort of concentration such as a visit to the theatre entails. Reading as a source of fiction also costs effort, whether financial or in the multiplicity of images we manufacture as we translate marks on paper into shapes in our minds. That then is the first hurdle.

To be in a position to learn anything we have to go through a series of stages. We have identified these as being attraction, attention, interest, involvement, concern, investment and obsession. So to start our drama, we have to find tasks that can equally attract a variety of pupils with different endowments. To move from attraction to attention is a huge step, bigger than from attention to interest. Each of these terms makes different demands and teaches differently. Attraction only demands that we let ourselves be distracted from what were doing before. Attention demands that we observe a bit what is going on. Interest means we start to bond ourselves a little with the situation, to bring a small part of experience to bear; while involvement suggests having a stake in the work and suppressing other distractions and behaviours. Concern means that things start to matter, that we have become bonded to outcomes; and when we are investing then we are putting in to the work a great amount of effort. Such investment can then lead to productive obsession and when children reach that stage they accost their teachers, they are empowered, they demand, they will not be said 'nay' for their energy is high and their play is joyful. Above all they create its future while the teacher tries to keep up sufficiently to enable things to continue progressing. A memory of ours is a mixed-ability group of 7-year-olds, on the hunt for an ill-intentioned powerful person who was poisoning Coca-Cola bottles at random, because he hated children. After a series of encounters with various slaves and acolytes, such as a Sun-bear of huge size, which guarded his chateau and was equipped with a silver transmitting claw; a crooked scientist using imprisoned students of science for the poisoning; a timid housekeeper who was frightened of the skeleton in the laboratory, he was finally confronted with his evil deeds just as he was feeding his little caged linnets with *chocolate!* Imagine a 7-year-old child issuing the following edict, it reminded us of the American Declaration of independence:

> You are an evil person, and you shall be destroyed and all your works in this evil house with you. You shall be taken to New York where you shall be justly judged and everything within this place shall be BURNED.

During this all the class are supporting the child as only a dedicated bonded group of friends can. That is when productive obsession is operating.

You can see in the account that along the way there has been a fair amount of science teaching. The human skeleton and all the placement of organs was made, and four basic experiments of science were tested (changing temperature, colour, volume and consistency), also experiments were made with codes, invisible ink and 'transmitting claws', needing close examination of bears' feet. We also had a look at linnets and their habits and the ingredients chocolate provided for their health! A fair amount of judgement had to operate about the trustworthiness of people's statements and their behaviour and predictions had to be made as to how evil people think and are likely to act when confronted by those bent on bringing them to justice.

But how can we pass on what we have learned about this progression from attraction to obsession? It has to be by practical example, so if we look at the hotel it might serve to identify principles that you can then translate to practice in other contexts. We wanted Maggie's people to become obsessed by running a hotel because it offered such a useful context for all their curriculum work and did so at different levels of difficulty, in addition to its group potential for deciding and caring about each other. Obviously whatever is the first attracting task it must be capable of arresting the attention of a mix of mobile, chairbound, alert and sleepy types, as well as engaging an age span of four years between the youngest and the eldest. There is no beginning to a hotel for it is not a story, it is a social phenomenon. All you can do is get a toe-hold into the culture of the place.

Attraction. A ground plan large enough to collect around, on a table with the short-sighted and chairbound stationed at the table edge and the others behind. This plan contained a hint of the shape of the hotel, the car park and adjoining main street. The management are considering planting trees around the car park to give shade to cars and to make the place look more attractive from the road. But these trees must not form a hazard to the parking of cars. So placing cut-out paper trees around a sheet of paper in the context of beauty, danger and shade was the first task – quite attractive because as trees are placed, they change the image and we can all see them doing it. The conceptual network might need a bit of embellishment for the less academically able. A few white spacing lines might be necessary to put on the chart to indicate territorial placement related with cars. You might also need a few car shapes to place between the white lines so that people who need more clues than talking it over can latch in there. Task one, then, breeds the potential to leave your car and walk over to the front door of the hotel. But what shall our hotel be called and how shall the sign look to arriving guests?

Attention. What are good letter shapes to be read at night; in bright sunlight; under artificial lights? We experiment with names, we screw up our eyes and try to read the words at a distance, we experiment with different sizes of letter and different formations and colour combinations. We finally select 'The Sundown Hotel' with its connotations of security, warmth and sleep, and a group paint the sign carefully, using rulers and colour combinations and a swirling logo in green.

Interest. We have kept the same point of view throughout the first two tasks, namely considering arriving guests and the impression they will have from the car park and the sign. Now we need personal interest, so we start on the problem of new uniforms for the staff, which must take account of age, rank, responsibility, the need to be recognised and to look nice no matter what build or colouring they are. We all put forward, via drawings, what we think; we discuss, share ideas and generally build through teacher negotiations so that it will be our hotel, we shall run it and be responsible for all that happens in regard to servicing our guests. Such vocabulary as 'I', 'we', 'when', starts to appear in teacher's statements like, 'Well, I don't know about you, but I don't think I suit bright yellow, but if that's the colour we all like then I'll go along with it.' Thus is 'now time' becoming acceptable. So uniforms are designed, selected and fabrics chosen for them. Porters frequently have to stand outside, cleaners must not knock things over when dusting, chefs do not let bits of their sleeves trail in soup, and so on. Decisions, decisions, and all recorded in memos, notes to suppliers, management at London headquarters, etc.

Involvement. (We're still running the place, remember.) Everyone has a work sheet, all clock in to work, all decide on tasks according to their interests. A lot of typists and cleaners come from the ladies, even the ordinarily mobile ones, and most of the gentlemen at this stage either run the bar or deal with security! Well, the rest of the staff must be somewhere else at this time. We start the actual work arranging the bar, bottles and collage, acquiring tools to dust and sweep and vacuum. We design the locks for doors and the rules for fire. We are actively creating and expressing that aspect of the hotel that is growing in our heads and the teacher is finding lots of problems suitable to these mental images. 'Where do you want the spare sheets putting, cleaners?' 'There's a person on the phone about delivering the fresh vegetables [the cash registers, the newspapers].' We are a cultural phenomenon. We have a hotel in operation.

Concern. We were 'gifted' with concern when Joan found a dead lady in 301, four lessons into the hotel. Concern takes many forms – not wanting to stop your own work and preferring to be told afterwards what happened; dropping everything and starting to move things forward; worrying about what time you'll arrive home tonight; taking all relevant evidence before the police arrive, and so on. The teacher is servicing all over the place, enabling a bit of suitable and necessary vocabulary, reporting to some typists what is going on on floor three, answering calls from anxious guests, or better still delegating others to 'try to soothe her' (she is the nervous lady in 302 who's heard all the bustle and is on the phone).

Investment. It is all very exciting but where do our priorities lie? With the dead lady? With our families who expect us home? With our clients who need lunch and taxis and services of all kinds? With the hotel managers? With the law? At the investment level people start to be able to lay aside need-interest and take on wider perceptions about action as social beings (Doris Lessings' *substance of we* feeling), even if they are not so exciting in appearance.

Obsession. This is the level when everyone wants to carry on with the hotel, and with as high a standard of suitable behaviour as possible. Selected behaviour, deliberately chosen for its purpose.

We now come to something that exercised all of us at first till we found some ways to solve it. This is the question of teachers finding material for their dramas. When there is a variety of skills and needs all under one roof, it looks a bit daunting to find material to suit the different levels. There is also the matter of treatment of the materials when found.

Most teachers feel themselves to be lacking in imagination, and they try to collect a bank of stories thinking that chronological events are what they will need. Drama doesn't work on stories though, it works on episodes, social encounters that reflect bondings between human beings and the ways they use power amongst themselves. You can teach yourself about this by considering how many episodes arise between waking up and arriving in school. An episode is an event that can be seen to be different in some way from what has just happened and what follows it. Waking up is a total episode because nothing that follows is at all like that first moment of awareness of the world. Getting up can span many more activities because they are all alike in that they prepare you for the public self that can meet others of your kind, or even the cat!

So into one episode would go washing, dressing, shaving (if you do). Breakfasting is another episode and so is opening the mail, even if they happen at the same time. In a drama based on the dual episodes of eating breakfast and opening letters, much will depend on what it is your primary intention to explore, express and use to create. Opening mail might be what the play is about and breakfast can be the context and location of action. If the play is about breakfasting while opening mail, then opening mail is the context and location of the action. You can invent what learning is going to be carried on the back of either of these by saying 'what is this about?' Breakfast can be about not wanting to go to work, or hating eggs and your wife, or being late for an interview, or being disappointed in love, or newly married. (There is a very exciting episode in Housman's play about Queen Victoria (*Victoria Regina*) when she watches her new husband, Albert, shaving; the first time she has seen him, or indeed any man, shave. Nothing happens outwardly except that Albert shaves and she marvels, but in the course of this it is understood (unhistorically) that the British royal family has almost married a scion of a royal house in which haemophilia is a factor.) The teacher can select episodes in human affairs that attract a class yet serve the teaching goals and the styles best suited to the class comfort. Now, *you* continue to discover episodes in going from bed to school ready to face the day and you will have many materials available. *You* invent the settings that can underlie them. By choosing what it is to be about, you introduce the bias and productive tension and make the action carry the meaning, just as in life. And above all, notice the amazing range of bondings it is possible to explore in the same episode.

You do not want all your drama material to be contemporary or domestic though, so you can easily learn, as we have done, to make it stretch around periods, locations and kinds of social events. You take any action in an event and you isolate one of its aspects. Let us take shaving, since we have mentioned it already. One aspect of shaving is *lather to ease* the removal of bristles from the chin. So when that is happening we could say that the person is 'of the brotherhood of all those who *make the way possible with least difficulty*'. Now recall all the stories you have ever read or heard; glance at today's paper, look at the garden, stroll around your house and you can find an infinite number of such examples. Here are a few to set you off;

1. priests administering extreme unction;
2. breaking some news with a cup of tea;
3. jilting someone with sensitivity;
4. administering anaesthetic for an operation;
5. making a will;
6. giving someone a map to help them on their way to find others who are lost;
7. joining the euthanasia society;
8. being a doorkeeper, secretary, footman, guardian;
9. being locksmiths;
10. carrying letters of credit;
11. knowing the password;
12. John the Baptist.

Now you can see how it works. You have spanned time, social hierarchy and context. You can now put in bias. What should be our responsibility in this episode, and what shall constitute the productive tension that makes it so important to people?

There is one last and most important matter. You have to stop trying to bring the action to completion so that the episode can be finished. The next few statements will be without any punctuation so you can realise what the pace is like in dramas where teacher and children try to reach the end. It is about shaving again! To be read at high speed, if possible becoming faster and faster. standbythewash-basingetthebrushlatherthesoapapplytoyourchinlookinmirrorpick-uprazorcheckbladesstartevencalmstrokesshakelatheroffrazorpat-drywashanddryrazorandface. You know it isn't like that in drama, but what is it like? Try to think of time not as a uniformly developing sequence but stretchable like humbug toffee, sometimes bunched up, sometimes long and thin, but the pattern always perceptible within the form, no matter from which viewpoint you examine it.

Let us take an example from our numbered list and see how such time might work. Let us select number 6 (giving someone a map to help them on their way to find others who are lost). First we set it in context. Who shall be lost? People from an oil rig in the North Sea. Who shall the class be? In other words what is their bias, their frame of reference? Let us say they service helicopters; they are part of a co-ordinated service to maintain safety in that area. The domain they enter will contain such things as these:

- how they communicate with others at distance;
- how they accomplish their work;
- who directs any changes of job, such as authorising them to make a rescue;
- how leadership is arranged;
- how they locate or find their way on such missions. And many more.

Now we can consider which of these aspects we shall make hurry along, or which we may even miss out altogether, and which we shall bunch up to become very dense for exploration. Which we decide upon depends entirely on what the teacher is trying to make the class to explore and hopefully to 'innerstand' and have new perceptions about. In the hotel, designing work clothes was a bunched-up experience because many of the children looked strange and we wanted the whole idea of our outer appearance and inner worth to be mulled over and have an airing, while we were apparently just designing some uniforms we would actually never make. This way of thinking about material and time stops every aspect of a situation having to have its own space. Some matters can, by agreement, be cut out altogether, others can be thoroughly explored. In the Coca-Cola saga we spent ages holed up by a prowling bear while we discussed how animals think. Likewise much time was spent in watching an evil scientist doing experiments and helping the frightened lady put the human model together (she really was hopeless and it gave us a lot of time to work it out for ourselves). But when it came to the final confrontation with the evil man we did not want to bother at all about how we would get into his private rooms except 'we'd be plumbers come to mend the pipes'. Take a look at any play, say *Hamlet* or *Julius Caesar*, and see which bits Shakespeare does not bother with either, then look at what he does with the situations he bunches up, like the death of Romeo and Juliet where we are forced to spend a long time in that family tomb and face every step of their final journey.

Every small episode has the potential to become a saga. You are in charge of your material and can work it to serve your ends in drama and your class's learning. When it comes to action upon the material remember Maggie's hotel car park. Do not go in for moving the furniture about, such as making pretend helicopters to repair by using desks. It might make a repair shop impossible. Designing places for storing spanners might be the best way of repairing helicopters. In our development of theme 6, we have explored a modern context, but what about finding your way by map to King Arthur's Court? And what kinds of persons have an interest in going there? Go on, you can do it from now on.

Finally, what kinds of equipment have we found to best help us in drama work? The prime resource is that of people and their experiences; living encyclopaedias of knowledge, memory and action potential. The next is materials that help images to be made and communicated around the group; all kinds of paper, writing and drawing materials suitable to your class's needs and related with their specialness. Your biggest problem, and it is the one all teachers face, is that when people discuss things there is often no record, visible and tangible, of what the whole experience is about. No record of ground covered, no resonance to give feedback or alter perspective. Putting images down, sharing in making such images, changing images by consultation, is essential in gaining group consensus and a position where everybody, no matter what the level of abstraction in their thinking, knows what is going on in the group endeavour. You can afford to be innovative and use those well tried materials, so sensible in infant rooms but sneered at in high schools (at least that is our experience), such as sand trays for quick modelling and diagramming.

When it comes to reference materials there is no end to what you can use and it is not all expensive. Any pictures of almost any kind become reference materials and you need the best encyclopaedias you can get. Likewise dictionaries. The problem with drama is that you never know which domains of knowledge you will be entering. This worried us at first and indeed still does because we never seem to know enough, but we are learning to cope without feeling so guilty. Maggie in a special school ran a circus in winter quarters and one minute needed to understand something of food for mynah birds, the next whether elephants had left and right feet. We have found drama starts more general knowledge questions going that demand immediate answers than anything else.

Throughout this paper we have assumed that your enthusiasm is like ours, strong enough to carry you through trial and error. If it was not at first, perhaps we have stimulated some interest. We have possibly raised more questions than the space we have can answer, but we believe that in teaching you just have to get in there and *give it a go*. We end our discussion with a few benefits we have observed in our classes since trying drama methods with our groups of mixed-ability children.

1. The children grew in confidence in expressing ideas orally to peers and adults (those who were known, e.g. teachers and also strangers, e.g. visitors). As a result of this, relationships with others improved.
2. Because the situations were to some extent controlled by the children, they had to accept responsibility for the way in which the work developed.
3. They were able to use their own ideas and interests.
4. They began to upgrade their spoken language and develop a sensitivity to the appropriate language for different occasions, e.g. formal/informal, solemn/lighthearted.
5. There was an opportunity to repeat and practise new found skills in a relevant situation.
6. The children began to experience the benefits of a willingness to work with others and learned to use the strengths of the group to compensate for individual weaknesses.
7. They became sufficiently self-confident to be able to admit to themselves and others that they did not always know the answer and were more likely as a result of this to rectify mistakes and seek information instead of covering up a lack of knowledge.
8. Some of the children talked about their work in Drama at home and parents were pressed into visiting school to see their work. One or two parents developed this interest at home in various ways.
9. One child became so enthusiastic that she made notes as she watched a programme about Celts at home. She also visited her local library and photocopied relevant material from reference books that that librarian produced at her request. (This child had come into the junior department of the school two years previously with a reading age of 6y 0m.)
10. There was a lot of communication about our work throughout and between schools and classes within schools.
11. Six months later children were able to remember and recall in great detail most of the things they had done.

12. Books and words connected with the drama work took on a special significance for the children.
13. There were occasions when recollections of their work generated an atmosphere that suggested that this shared experience was special to them and important, even long after the event.

Educational use of drama has a long way to travel. Do join us on the journey.

—3

Physical Education and Dance

Patricia Sanderson

Dance, an essentially artistic activity, is readily acknowledged as contributing to aesthetic and creative education. Physical education (PE) activities, on the other hand, are less frequently regarded in this way, yet the importance of aesthetic and creative experiences to the participant and spectator of gymnastics, games, swimming and other sports, is evident. These are therefore important aspects of both PE and dance, which are integrated with the physical, emotional, social and cognitive dimensions, providing a valuable means of all round education that is accessible to all children.

THE VALUE OF PHYSICAL EDUCATION AND DANCE

Physical activity plays a crucial rôle in a child's satisfactory development. The work of Piaget and others has established the relationship between adequate sensori–motor experiences in the early years and later cognitive growth, and it is widely recognised that involvement in a range of perceptual–motor and imaginative play activities is of major importance in the sound integrated development of young children.

Yet in today's society, opportunities for physical activity are becoming increasingly restricted for many children. Research by Cherrington (1980) for the Leverhulme Foundation, for example, showed that the motor development of children raised in high-rise flats was significantly lower than for those raised in ordinary homes. Equally disturbing is the trend of many families towards predominantly sedentary lifestyles where watching television is the major recreational pursuit and cars reduce the necessity to walk very far. Escalation in traffic in recent years has resulted in the virtual disappearance of street games, once a common feature of British life, and sadly these games are rarely seen in the school playground either. Parents are unwilling to allow unsupervised play in parks and other open spaces and although more public swimming pools have been built in recent years there are many children who are unable to use these facilities because of a disability or lack of financial resources. Recent research at both Lough-borough University (Dickinson, 1986) and at Exeter University (Armstrong, 1987) confirms the limited amount of physical activity among children outside school time.

Physical education and dance lessons therefore assume particular significance in the promotion of the satisfactory all-round development of children, especially for those with special educational needs whose difficulties could well be exacerbated and in some cases caused by their restricted environments. It is necessary for schools to compensate by regularly providing structured experiences in PE and dance throughout the nursery and primary years.

In this chapter the emphasis will be on the practical involvement of the child in PE and dance activities, thereby acknowledging the fundamental contribution of physical activity to satisfactory physical, social, emotional, cognitive, aesthetic and creative development. This does not underestimate, however, the importance of observation as a learning experience, particularly for those with special educational needs. The rôles of participant and observer are closely linked and this will be stressed throughout.

Physical development

Physical activity is vitally important for the normal growth of bones and muscle tissue, for fitness, strength and mobility. Given an adequate diet, children who participate in regular vigorous activity are typically not only fit and strong but also more alert, more aware, stimulated by and interested in their surroundings. This general feeling of well-being is important for effective learning to take place and children with learning difficulties, especially the subdued and withdrawn, could benefit considerably from the invigorating effects of regular exercise.

Children with physical or sensory disabilities often need encouragement to participate fully in PE activities. Over-protection by parents and teachers has frequently given rise to the erroneous assumption that participation is inadvisable, consequently many of these children are extremely unfit and overweight and limbs that are mobile are often very weak. Involvement in PE and dance activities is therefore of particular importance for children with disabilities.

Gymnastics develops strength and mobility, energetic games improve cardio-vascular efficiency and swimming is invaluable in providing not only excellent all-round exercise but also independent mobility. For the extremely anxious or nervous child who is intimidated by apparatus, water or the more boisterous PE situation in general, the vigorous rhythmic movement of dance lessons may be a particularly appropriate means of achieving physical fitness.

Emotional development

For satisfactory emotional development a positive self-image is of crucial importance and a fundamental factor in the child's acquisition of a confident view of her or himself is the degree of success achieved in school. For many children with learning difficulties PE and dance can play a most important rôle as it is an area of the curriculum in which all children can experience success, achieve status with their peers and merit genuine praise. Creative dance, where the emphasis is on individual interpretation and the quality of the movement response, can help develop confidence. In many aspects of PE the teacher must set individually attainable tasks so that success is assured.

The acquisition of perceptual–motor skills is important for the growth of self-confidence and esteem. The rate of development of such skills varies greatly but children who have had restricted opportunities for play and for handling apparatus can be clumsy. Lack of body awareness (indicated by, for example, regularly bumping into others, knocking over equipment or tripping up) and poor hand–eye co-ordination (for example, difficulty in throwing, catching and hitting) can cause great distress to a child. Morris and Whiting (1971) point out that there are a number of studies linking clumsiness with behaviour disturbance, underlining the emphasis that should be placed in the nursery and primary schools on the improvement of perceptual–motor skills.

The opportunity for the physical release of emotional tension is also a valuable aspect of participation in PE and dance for children with behaviour difficulties. Aggressive feelings and emotions can be given an outlet, most obviously in expressive dance, which is also the safest medium as no equipment is involved. However, within carefully structured and supervised games and gymnastics situations, there are numerous and obvious possibilities for the release of tension and physical energy.

For physically disabled children, developing a positive self-image is related to correcting an overly negative view of their abilities while coming to terms with what their bodies can and cannot do. Children with sight impairments have limited body awareness and so gymnastics and dance are particularly useful in helping to develop body concept and consequently self-image. The concept of the body in relation to space that is above, behind, near and far, must also be developed in order to reduce the vulnerability and disorientation experienced by these children.

Social development

Physical education and dance can play a fundamental part in a child's social development by helping to promote co-ordination, strength, fitness and skill. These attributes are of major importance in enabling a child to join successfully with others in recreational activities. Many children who are rejected at play can become withdrawn, defensive and aggressive.

By means of PE and dance, teachers can also help children learn how to play with others, to co-operate, to share equipment and ideas, take turns and learn to accept defeat, while realising the need to persevere to attain success. It is important therefore that games lessons should stress co-operation between participants as well as competition. Partner and group work in dance may be a particularly useful means of encouraging withdrawn children to become involved because of the absence of competition. Similarly for some children who have become isolated, owing perhaps to a physical disability, participation in dance lessons can be an initial means of making contact with others. Inhibitions can sometimes be broken down more easily and integration promoted when movement is the sole medium with any barriers or anxieties relating to apparatus removed.

Cognitive development

The relationship between perceptual–motor experience and cognitive development has been the focus of a considerable amount of research in recent years, particularly in the USA. Kephart (1960) for example, in his influential book *The Slow Learner in the Classroom*, stresses the importance of additional movement experiences for those children whose limited environments and lifestyles have failed to provide them with the sensori–motor experiences necessary to establish the 'readiness' or basic skills that are prerequisites for the development of the complex activities of reading, writing and arithmetic. For instance, before eye–hand co-ordination can develop, a child must first be able to distinguish right and left sides of the body and control two sides separately and simultaneously. These factors are also related to reading readiness.

In more general terms the psychologist Cratty (1974) has pointed out that PE and dance lessons are likely to have greatest impact on overall intellectual functioning if the teaching approach ensures that the child is actively involved in decision-making, devising solutions to problems, contributing something. The strong motivating effect on classroom learning of success in movement classes, the improvement in self-image and in social relationships, and the feeling of well-being and alertness resulting from participation in physical activities, should also be borne in mind.

Physical education and dance experiences can also be very helpful for those children who have difficulty in forming concepts because of problems in integrating information from different senses. For instance, exploration in movement of spatial concepts such as bigger and smaller, higher and lower, forwards, backwards and sideways, has been found to promote understanding of the appropriate verbal and written symbols. The additional information supplied by the kinaesthetic receptors in muscles and joints can be particularly valuable too, for children with sensory disabilities.

Aesthetic development

Given the importance of PE and dance experiences in physical, emotional, social and cognitive development, it is fortunate that children find movement itself intrinsically pleasurable. Enjoyable sensations arise from running, jumping, rolling, climbing, swimming, moving rhythmically to music, throwing, catching, hitting the ball, and so on. Many children from deprived environments or with restricted lifestyles have limited knowledge of the joy and delight found in running freely in large spaces or the tactile pleasures of moving through water or rolling down a grassy bank. The possibilities for immediate aesthetic pleasures in PE and dance activities are vast and open to all children regardless of ability or background. The simplest movement can provide sensations and feelings that give great enjoyment to a child and, as skill and sensitivity develop, the teacher can present further opportunities for more refined and extensive aesthetic experiences. The delight in the initial acquisition of a skill such as catching a ball, moving in harmony with a musical rhythm, becoming waterborne, or completing a forward roll can be re-created in the persistent repetition that fascinates young children. Subsequently, satisfaction is gained in constructing sequences in gymnastics and dance, inventing a new game and being part of a team or group when co-operation produces a good performance. For many children such feelings of aesthetic pleasure are rare and the opportunities to experience them in PE and dance should not be easily dismissed nor the value of such a source of aesthetic knowledge and experience be underestimated. Many teachers, for instance, report that movement lessons are the first occasions when some children smile.

Aesthetic sensibilities awakened by means of movement experiences can be enhanced by encouraging children to become more alert to visual aesthetic qualities in dance and sport. Watching each other perform well-executed gymnastics or dance sequences, observing a game well played, appreciating the performance of a dance company in a theatre, can all promote aesthetic awareness and interest. Participating in and watching physical education and dance activities can make children more conscious of aesthetic qualities such as beauty, grace, strength, power, shape, line, and help them acquire fundamental aesthetic concepts of form and expression.

Creative development

The growth of aesthetic understanding is closely associated with creative development in PE and dance. Children discover how different parts of the body move in relation to each other and how contrasting rhythms, dynamics, patterns and pathways can be combined in very many different ways to give very different results. Encounters with a range of equipment and apparatus stimulate the learning of new skills, extending the potential for additional creative experiences. Opportunities to devise games, gymnastic sequences and dances give insight into the creative process, which involves experimentation, selection and rejection before movements can be combined into a satisfying whole.

Such creative experiences are open to all children. Physically disabled children, notwithstanding a limited movement range, can produce very original, well-structured movement phrases and devise interesting, demanding games, involving themselves and other children. It is also often the case that children who have difficulties with verbal or written language symbols thrive when given the opportunity to be inventive in the medium of movement. These children often surprise their teachers with the individuality of their responses and the complexity of the forms they construct. Dance is particularly valuable for those children who are frustrated by a limited facility with the spoken or written word (frustration that can lead to behaviour disturbance), enabling them to express and communicate feelings and ideas through an alternative medium.

Participation in dances or games that are already established, that is, devised by others including the teacher, have a part to play in developing understanding of the creative process, for it is important that children experience a complete structure, an end-product. Physical involvement in a whole game, dance or gymnastics sequence helps a child understand how parts fit together to form a whole, thus acquiring crucial knowledge relating to the key concepts of structure and form, and clarifying what is meant by 'a game', 'a dance', 'a phrase', 'a sequence' and so on. Information obtained by the child in the rôle of spectator makes similar contributions to his or her creative development. Such concrete experiences are an important part of learning in the creative domain for all children, but particularly for those who have difficulty in making connections and seeing relationships. Creative interpretation, however, whether as performer or observer, does not appear to be directly related to intellectual skills and can often compensate for limited physical abilities too. We are all aware of the child who gains an advantage over someone more technically skilful or intellectually gifted by an inventive approach to a game; or the dancer whose expressive qualities overcome other limitations. These are important aspects of creative understanding that should be borne in mind by the teacher of children with special educational needs.

SUMMARY

It is apparent that regular PE and dance lessons, where the child is periodically creator, performer and viewer, can make important contributions to all-round development and therefore such participation is of great value to the child with special needs. Primary school teachers frequently remark on the positive effects that PE and dance experiences can have on a child's general attitude and overall progress. The following anecdotes are examples.

Leela had a physical disability and used a walking aid. When she joined an infant class in her local school she was immature for her age and had been over-protected, particularly as far as any physical exertion was concerned. Consequently Leela was overweight, her perceptual–motor skills were poorly developed and she was rather isolated in the playground. Despite her initial reluctance to participate in any PE, the teacher gradually persuaded her to join in that part of the gymnastics lesson when the large apparatus could give her physical support and the thick mats reassurance that she would not be hurt. Almost immediately Leela found great delight in exploring the apparatus and surprised herself with her own achievements. She discovered the pleasure of moving, of finding out what her body could do, whereas, up to that point, her preoccupation and that of others had been with what it could not do. Confidence, fitness, strength and co-ordination all gradually improved. As the year proceeded Leela became integrated into the class and her walking aid was accepted both by herself and other children as part of her, rather than seen as a barrier, which is how it had been regarded hitherto. Her alert, bright demeanour affected her overall attitude to school, she became more interested in classroom work and at home was much more independent.

Michael was another example. He had learning difficulties in most curriculum areas, as his verbal and written skills were poor and his concentration limited causing him to be disruptive in the classroom. On entering the junior school, Michael was introduced to expressive dance experiences and from the start enjoyed the vigorous rhythmic activity, which seemed to release tension in him, especially when music was also employed. Michael was also found to be very imaginative in movement, he had good ideas that he was able to express in a dance form. Consequently he was often asked to demonstrate for his fellow pupils and to be part of school performances. Michael blossomed as a result, his new-found status improved his relationships with others, he became more co-operative in general and began to take a greater interest in other subjects.

AIMS

The overall aim of PE and dance in the primary school is the integrated physical, social, emotional, cognitive, aesthetic and creative development of the child. It is clear that potentially a child with special needs can benefit in all these ways from participation in physical activities, although teaching methods and curriculum content will also have a significant bearing on achievements.

Teaching approaches

In order to help children learn, teachers must be imaginative and flexible in their approaches, the more so if there are those with special educational needs in the class. Teacher intervention can be both direct and indirect and, although the stress in PE and dance in primary schools is on the latter, there is room for both approaches, emphases varying both within and between lessons according to the needs of individuals and the immediate objectives of the teacher.

For the most part the teacher is in the rôle of initiator and guide, taking as a starting point what a child can do rather than focusing on a specific end product. Children respond individually within the limitations of tasks set by the teacher and in this way a child can grow in confidence and independence. Personal interpretation is valued and skill develops gradually along with awareness of qualitative aspects of movement and inventiveness. This informal situation, whereby children are given opportunities to think for themselves, to explore and experiment, can greatly benefit children who are inhibited by tension and anxiety (often due to memories of frequent failure) if asked to conform to a precise way of moving.

Because progress is individual, all children can experience success. In order to stimulate children to improve their movement responses and therefore become more skilful, and to help them create novel, well-structured sequences, games or dances, a teacher calls upon a variety of techniques including demonstrations, questions, suggestions and comments. A child with a specific educational need may respond more positively to one particular technique rather than another and therefore a teacher needs to be aware of not only the potential for learning in each technique, whether used separately and in combination, but also the needs of the individual.

Demonstrations by the teacher, by children or by means of videotape-recordings are powerful means of communicating information and capturing interest and attention. In particular, children with learning difficulties can benefit more readily from moving visual images than from verbal explanations. If children are being asked to notice aspects of a performance, then the demonstration must be of a limited length and of good quality for the same reasons that blackboard work should always be of a high standard. A child might be asked to demonstrate in order to motivate him, raise his morale or integrate him more into the class. Obviously any demonstration must be relevant and a good illustration of a particular point, otherwise the child could be open to ridicule with serious consequences for personal development. It needs to be stressed, however, that a valuable demonstration should not be interpreted as comprising spectacular movement. The originality of the work or the careful execution could well be aspects to which attention is being drawn.

Questions are important means of focusing a child's attention and helping his concentration, thereby avoiding the onset of the aimless behaviour that often precedes disruptive incidents. Questions can greatly assist learning when they are associated with a demonstration or when a child is working independently; they can challenge to greater effort, inventiveness and clarification. A teacher's suggestions also have a place in encouraging creative work by initiating exploration or stimulating the imagination, thereby engendering confidence and feelings of security among some children. On the other hand, care must be taken to avoid suppressing independence in the insecure child or one whose lack of confidence makes her reluctant to offer her own ideas when those of the teacher automatically appear to be far superior.

Underpinning all teaching, of course, should be the regular praise and encouragement that most children need, but especially those for whom progess is slow. Whenever possible comments should be positive, although favourable remarks should always be followed by a challenging question or suggestion, the aim constantly being to improve a response and expand awareness. The broad analysis of movement usually attributed to Rudolf Laban is a useful aid to the teacher. This analysis draws attention to the major constituents of movement – namely the body moving in space, with varying dynamics, in relation to other people, apparatus or equipment. Thus when observing a child a teacher might consider:

• what the body is doing and which parts are being used;
• where the movement is going in the space;
• how the movement is accomplished, that is, the dynamic quality;
• with whom or what the movement is accomplished.

A teacher with this summary at the forefront of his mind can more readily help a child by analysing the movements and seeing more precisely where assistance is needed, whether this is in the accurate performance of a skill or a more imaginative interpretation of a task.

This analysis and the techniques referred to can also be usefully employed when a direct, precise method of teaching is called for as, for example, when safety factors are involved. Children must be shown the correct way to lift and carry apparatus, and must learn to land and roll safely so that injury is avoided. Direct intervention by the teacher is also sometimes necessary for the acquisition of other fundamental skills such as taking the weight on the hands or travelling to a specific rhythm. Occasionally it is appropriate to manipulate a child through a movement physically, a swimming stroke for example, as this may be the only means whereby the child can gain relevant kinaesthetic information and experience the feelings associated with completing a movement correctly. If a physically disabled child is involved, a teacher must, of course, be scrupulously familiar with the child's limitations and potential capabilities.

Direct teaching may involve the whole class, although here the maturity of the children is a factor. Juniors respond positively to fairly extensive periods of formal teaching, whereas with infants, whose concentration is much shorter, this kind of intervention must necessarily be brief and interspersed with periods of exploration and experimentation. For the most part, a direct approach will be used by the teacher when dealing with individuals. Children with learning difficulties, for example, benefit considerably as the teacher can ensure that incidental information, which such children often fail to pick up, is recognised and absorbed. Emotionally disturbed children also enjoy the security of this approach.

Working towards a narrow, clearly-specified goal can also give a sense of purpose to many children; and when success is achieved it can be readily acknowledged as it conforms to a recognisable model.

The positive effects in terms of motivation and self-image are enormous, and of great importance to children for whom success is not a regular occurrence in other areas of the curriculum. On the other hand, the possibility of failure is ever present, with its dire consequences. The teacher must therefore ensure that the child does succeed, either by modifying the objectives or breaking down the skill and setting intermediate, achievable goals.

A judicious combination of direct and indirect methods of teaching PE and dance activities is most likely to help a child's physical, emotional, social, cognitive, aesthetic and creative development.

THE PHYSICAL EDUCATION CURRICULUM

In primary schools the PE curriculum generally comprises gymnastics, games and swimming. Other physical activities, for instance athletics and various outdoor pursuits, obviously make important contributions to all-round development, including the aesthetic and creative. Unfortunately, both lack of time in the school day and access to suitable facilities prevent the regular appearance of these and other activities on the timetable. This section therefore focuses on gymnastics, games and swimming as providing the most consistent opportunities for children, including those with special educational needs, to gain experiences that will promote integrated growth. Each aspect of the curriculum makes specific as well as general contributions to all-round development.

Gymnastics

Gymnastics is concerned with the control and management of the body, when co-ordination, strength, mobility and flexibility can all be improved. Perceptual–motor skills develop as children explore how their bodies can move, particularly when large apparatus is involved. As skill increases, so too do opportunities for aesthetic experiences. Enhanced body awareness leads to further experimentation, combining and varying basic skills into sequences of movement. Growth in understanding of space, time and weight open up the possibility of further aesthetic and creative experiences.

The teaching material of gymnastics is comprised essentially of body actions. Such actions include ways of travelling on the feet, on hands and feet, by rolling, climbing, pushing and pulling; jumping and landing safely; stillness and balance; swinging and hanging from apparatus; taking the weight mainly on the hands, and so on. Familiarising children with contrasting dynamics, namely strength and lightness, suddenness and sustainment, can add quality and interest to their movement. Similarly awareness of space in terms of variations in level, focus, direction, and quantity, enriches the gymnastics experience.

Gymnastics lessons for children in nursery and infant schools should provide extensive opportunities for the perceptual–motor experiences that are essential for continued satisfactory progress. The objective, therefore should be the acquisition of a pool of basic skills gained from exploration of body actions in relation to dynamic and spatial factors. The creative process is introduced by expecting children to link together two or three movements, such as a jump, a good landing and a roll, to form a short phrase. Apparatus enables children to develop further skills as they learn to lift, carry and place it safely, explore all its possibilities for travelling, jumping, swinging, hanging and so on, then to control the body safely as it returns to the floor. Progressions of apparatus for young children are straightforward, namely mats and benches developing to stools, tables, climbing frame and ropes.

Children of junior school age who are able to build on this wide experience are usually ready to explore a specific area of movement in greater depth via a 'theme', experimenting with taking the weight on the hands for instance. Children of this age should also be able to vary spatial and dynamic dimensions to construct increasingly complex phrases and sequences. Similar ways of working should be evident during the apparatus section, with equipment organised to provide the necessary stimuli and challenges.

These are the general indicators of broad stages of development in gymnastics and children of all needs and abilities are capable of progressing along these lines, given an environment that provides regular, structured lessons. When limited previous experience has restricted the development of body management and general movement awareness, then those concerned need to be given the time to explore and experiment to gather that fundamental pool of movement experiences. As the overall teaching approach is informal, tasks can be framed for individuals as the need arises and personal attention given so that progress is assured.

Well-structured lessons with clear objectives are essential if children are to gain maximum benefit from gymnastic experiences. A lesson usually consists of three sections, a brief opening activity, followed by a period of floor work and finally the use of apparatus. In a 40-minute lesson the first two or three minutes are usually spent on gradually warming up the body to reduce injury risk from the onset of sudden strenuous activity. This is a particularly important consideration in relation to children who have physical disabilities and are therefore less active than other children for most of the day.

The beginning of the lesson also attunes the children to the nature of the activity that is to take place, including its rules and routines, so that discipline is established at the outset. The second stage lasts approximately ten minutes and gives opportunities, by means of a mixture of direct and indirect teaching methods, to explore, experiment, select, improve and consolidate according to individual needs and within the restrictions set by the teacher. The final part usually involves apparatus, and as the lifting, carrying and placing of equipment constitute important experiences for children time must be allowed both to bring it out and to put it away carefully. Apparatus should be arranged by the teacher in accordance with the objectives of the lesson: that is why the practice in some schools of having one single apparatus arrangement for every class, regardless of age or background, places serious limitations on the potential value of gymnastic experiences. Additionally, of course, children in those circumstances are denied opportunities for important perceptual–motor and other experiences because of lack of floor work and the handling of equipment. Apparatus should be arranged to suit the needs of the class as a whole and of individuals, in order to stimulate, encourage and challenge. In this part of the lesson the children work in small groups. This gives opportunities for children with varying needs and levels of achievement, boys and girls, to work together, co-operating, helping and learning from each other.

Games

The primary school years are crucially important for the development of basic games skills, for without these skills children can find it increasingly difficult to join in play activities with others and in some cases, the ensuing feelings of rejection and exclusion can lead to behaviour problems, particularly if a child also has learning difficulties in the classroom. Co-ordination, especially hand–eye co-ordination as in throwing and catching, and the manipulation of various implements such as bats and sticks, are fundamental to successful participation. Acquiring the concept of a game, realising the necessity for structure and rules is also essential. Children with learning difficulties are often very good at acquiring particular skills but may need help in working with a partner or as a member of a team and in comprehending what is meant by co-operation, fair competition and, in the case of upper juniors, tactics. It is vital that these basic skills and understanding are acquired during the primary school years for the secondary school stage is too late for many and in consequence an enjoyable and accessible means of keeping fit, recreation and social interaction, is denied such children. Games lessons are potential sources of extensive aesthetic and creative experiences too, particularly for children whose restricted environments or disabilities have limited their skill development or their encounters with open spaces. A games lesson taken outside on a bright sunny day can be an uplifting experience, although the converse should also be borne in mind. There are many for whom enduring long, tedious lessons in cold, damp conditions ensured that henceforth games were to be avoided at all costs.

Games teaching is concerned fundamentally with the acquisition of basic skills and an understanding of what is meant by playing a game. Skills include running, jumping, dodging, marking, throwing, catching, kicking, heading, dribbling, serving, bowling, hitting, rolling, bouncing, aiming, trapping, intercepting, tackling and fielding. Whenever it is appropriate, skills should be introduced without the relevant hand-held implement, bouncing a ball with the hand for instance before involving the manipulating of a bat. However, extensive experience should be given with a wide range of equipment including various types of bats, such as table-tennis, padder tennis and cricket bats, shinty sticks, quoits and of course balls of different sizes and weights. Equipment should be available in contrasting shapes, sizes, textures and colours, to suit the needs of individuals, to attract a child's curiosity and to maintain his interest – all important considerations, particularly when the attention span is short.

The rate of skill development of individuals varies enormously, therefore the teacher must be constantly on the alert, breaking down skills into stages as necessary, ensuring that success is achieved and frustration minimised. With regular practice, the basic skills can be acquired by all children and the teacher must ensure that they are given the necessary opportunities to explore and experiment alone, with a partner or with the teacher so that steady progress can be made. Full-size adult games are inappropriate for children of primary school age. Games for two to five children are preferable as everyone can be involved most of the time and children with varying needs can more easily be accommodated. The rules, overall structure, size of the pitch, equipment, should all be simple and related to the needs of the group. Numerous relevant games are readily available in the curriculum literature, or the teacher can easily devise one specifically for a group. Junior children can invent their own activities, within limitations set by the teacher in terms of equipment, size of pitch or rules. When children of different abilities are included in the group then the members themselves must find ways of incorporating everyone. Variation within the group must not be too great however, otherwise frustration is likely to be the outcome for all concerned.

The key to successful games teaching is good organisation. If the rhythm of the lesson is constantly interrupted because of lack of sufficient equipment, for example, then the attention and interest of some children will be lost quickly and the teacher's energy wasted in vainly attempting to regain their interest. Equipment should be appropriate for both the activity and the needs of individuals. For instance a child who is unco-ordinated and clumsy, or hyperactive, or who has a specific disability should be provided, at least initially, with a large ball and not a small, light, bouncy one. All apparatus should be classified according to type and colour, with boxes of equipment easily identified and labelled to promote reading skills.

Children should also be involved in organisational processes whenever possible. Individuals should be expected to collect and return their own piece of equipment; in other instances children can be given responsibilities involving collecting, counting, checking and returning apparatus. Good organisation should also be evident in the selection and preparation of the playing area. For instance, using markers to reduce the space so that every child is always within sight and hailing distance; noting the location of windows and boundary fences so that appropriate activities can be chosen and the needs of individuals taken into account. The weather is also an important consideration, particularly when the less mobile or poorly co-ordinated are involved.

The format of a games lesson follows a familiar pattern, namely introductory warm-up activity, then the practice of basic skills and finally the application of those skills into small games. This basic structure is sufficiently flexible to take into consideration such variables as the weather and also to maintain the interest of everyone in the class. A mixture of direct and indirect methods should be employed, involving various teaching techniques. Demonstrations are particularly valuable in showing precisely the components of a skill or indicating clearly the organisation of a game.

The teacher's overriding objective with children in the nursery and infant school should be to develop the basic skills, including the manipulation of a wide range of implements. A young child should also have an understanding of what is involved in playing a game, including co-operation, rules and simple structures. Thereafter, skill should gradually increase so that longer repetitive sequences are possible, such as bouncing or dribbling a ball, hitting a ball against the wall, and so on. Various combinations of skills, including bouncing and hitting, dribbling and aiming, as well as the invention of sequences, should be the next target. Children of junior school age should be expected to co-operate in small groups in the playing of a game as well as be capable of inventing their own games activities.

Swimming

Swimming provides excellent all-round exercise and can be enjoyed by virtually everyone regardless of cognitive or physical ability. Most children become waterborne quickly and subsequently find great pleasure in moving independently through water. As the island on which we live provides not only ready access to the sea but also an abundance of rivers, lakes, canals and ponds, the ability to survive in water is essential and children should be taught to swim as early as possible in the nursery or infant school. Swimming is also the most popular physical recreation activity among both children and adults and so a child is at a great disadvantage socially if she cannot swim. Inability to swim also excludes participation in a wide range of associated activities including sailing, canoeing, surfing, water-skiing and so on.

Along with most other physical skills, swimming is more difficult to learn for an adolescent or adult, as many will testify, and this is likely to be more so for those with special educational needs. It is important, therefore, that all children are taught to swim at primary-school age. Everyone should be given the opportunity to take advantage of this activity, which can not only provide an excellent means of exercise, pleasure, recreation and social interaction throughout life, but also has survival value.

The swimming pool, however, is a potentially hazardous environment and so it is crucial that appropriate safety measures are implemented by the teacher and understood by all the children. It is particularly important that those children with learning difficulties or behaviour problems realise that water offers possibilities not only for great fun but also great danger if not treated with due caution and respect. Rules and routines must therefore be strictly adhered to at all times.

In order to take charge of a class, a teacher must have a RLSS Bronze Life-Saving medal, although most LEAs have their own qualified instructors, leaving the teacher free to give individual attention to any child with special needs. In certain cases it is necessary to have extra help; a child with severe behaviour problems, for example, would need the constant attention of a teacher, while a serious physical disability demands special expertise on the part of the teacher so that there is no possibility of injury as a result of mishandling. Most LEAs also have their own safety regulations, including those relating to children with special needs, and these too must be complied with. Although responsibility for teaching may in some cases lie with the LEA instructors, a teacher should be in overall control of the class and ensure that everyone is familiar with expected patterns of behaviour. For instance, shouting, running along the bath-side, jumping in the water without permission, pushing, splashing and so on, must all be strictly forbidden.

The class teacher should also inform any LEA instructor of the special needs of individual children, particularly when those needs may not be immediately apparent. For instance, pupils with ear ailments should be excluded from jumping, diving or underwater swimming and partially sighted children need the permission of a consultant ophthalmologist. Some children with physical disabilities could tire easily and feel the cold quickly. Very timid beginners or those making initial slow progress could also become cold, but if the lesson is cut short for these children the teacher should ensure that they are adequately supervised in the changing rooms.

The teacher is normally at the side of the pool, visible to all bathers and in turn able to keep everyone in view, counting heads occasionally as an extra precaution. In addition, those children likely to experience difficulties in swimming could all wear caps of the same easily identifiable colour. Children should be loosely grouped according to their stage of progress and allocated to different parts of the pool so that identification of individuals can easily be made. It is also an important safety consideration that the pool is not overcrowded, so that children can practise without too much splashing, which can intimidate the apprehensive and excite others leading to over-boisterous behaviour.

Strict adherence to basic rules and routines is therefore crucial so that the swimming lesson is conducted safely and with maximum benefit to all. A well-ordered lesson also means that those who need individual attention can be given it. However, it is also important that children are not fearful; on the contrary the teacher's approach should be that swimming is fun. Children should be relaxed and happy but not over-excited as this could obviously be dangerous.

There are clearly identifiable stages of progress in swimming and the teacher's objectives will vary according to the needs of individuals. Initially time should be given for familiarisation with the facilities, changing, methods of entering and leaving the water and other fundamentals. Confidence in the water is an absolute priority and children must learn to relax with the head under the water and eyes open, so that panic does not occur whenever water covers the face. It is also vital that correct breathing is established, by blowing bubbles across the surface for instance, so that water is not taken in through the nose, which can be particularly distressing. Buoyancy is the next objective and it is an enormous thrill when the feet are lifted from the pool bottom with or without a swimming aid. Realisation that the natural buoyancy of the body increases when air fills the lungs is an important further stage. Incidentally, it is obvious that swimming offers many opportunities for the practical exposition of a number of scientific principles and this can assist the understanding of fundamental concepts, especially among children with learning difficulties.

These basic aspects of learning to swim, namely confidence and buoyancy, are crucial to survival and also to successful subsequent learning. Each child should therefore be helped to reach this level of competence and imaginative teaching methods should be employed to ensure that this does happen. Group activities, for instance, can be great fun and also present opportunities for children with varying needs and abilities to work together, helping each other and taking various responsibilities. Equipment should be colourful, of varying shapes and of tactile interest to help maintain the concentration of those whose attention is limited, to motivate and to encourage perseverance. Once confidence has been gained, children can begin to try their own strokes before being introduced to breaststroke, backstroke or crawl depending upon their natural inclinations. A 'whole stroke' approach, that is learning to do arms and leg stroke together, then practising each separately rather than the reverse, is considered superior and is also more fun. A mixture of direct and indirect teaching methods, verbal and visual explanations should be employed, tailored to the needs of a particular group or individual. Physical guidance of the learner through the correct stroke is useful, ideally in the water if a teacher is available. If children can see the full stroke on a videotape that too is helpful; otherwise charts can be useful.

For infants, ten minutes in the water is sufficient, for juniors 30 minutes is a typical length of lesson, although this can obviously be varied as necessary to suit individuals. Groups should be organised before the lesson begins according to needs and abilities and children should know where they will be working in the pool. Entrance to the pool should be orderly and the immediate practice of a previously experienced activity should follow so that there is no opportunity for children to misbehave, become too cold, or be bored. The major portion of the lesson is spent on the introduction of new activities and the improvement of strokes and includes both individual and group work. The lesson may end with free practice and more able pupils can spend time on gymnastic skills underwater such as handstands, collecting bricks, swimming through hoops and so on.

In terms of making progress in swimming, a block of lessons, for example once every day for three weeks, is better than fifteen lessons spread over a term and the aim should be for all children to learn to swim in that period. This point is particularly relevant for those children who have difficulty in remembering precise experiences from week to week. Stages in swimming are clearly identified, that is, confidence in the water; becoming waterborne with and then without buoyancy aids; moving through the water on the front and back; acquisition of technically accurate and efficient swimming strokes; jumping into the water leading to a plain header from the side. These stages of progress are readily recognisable by both the child and the teacher. Reaching each stage is itself a strong motivator to further efforts and an enormous boost to confidence. Children can keep their own record of progress or achievements can be recognised by a swimming award, a badge or a braid, for simple swimming skills through to distance and speed swimming. LEAs often have their own award systems that can be employed and there are national awards such as those of the ASA and RLSS, but perhaps it is more appropriate in primary schools if each school devises its own system so that each child is competing only with himself and everyone can gain an award. For children with learning difficulties in the classroom, or who have other special needs, the achievement of a badge that can be worn and displayed for others to see can have profound positive repercussions.

THE DANCE CURRICULUM

The potential of dance experience for integrated all-round development has not yet been fully realised in the primary school. For instance dance can be a vigorous physical activity promoting fitness, strength, mobility, releasing tensions and providing a useful means of assisting social development. The particular value of dance experience however lies in the possibilities for aesthetic and creative education, by giving children opportunities to acquire a wide range of expressive movements, and to compose, perform and watch dances. Most importantly such experiences are open to all children, whatever their cognitive or physical abilities, providing an alternative means of expression and communication of feelings and ideas, to the written or spoken word.

All children enjoy rhythmic expressive movement in the rôles of both participant and observer. For large numbers this interest continues into adulthood where dancing is an immensely popular pastime. Teachers should therefore capitalise on this inherent interest in movement for its own sake and use it as a base from which to expand children's aesthetic and creative understanding. The restricted environments and lifestyles of many children mean that they could very well be unaware of the possibilities lying beyond the dance seen in discotheques or on television 'pop' shows, yet dance is an immensely rich and varied area to explore, comprising a wide range of theatre, recreational, social and national dance forms.

In order to introduce children to this world, teachers in primary schools must themselves broaden their own concept of dance in education. For many teachers the dance curriculum is comprised solely of a practical exploration of Rudolf Laban's analysis of movement. Typically a stimulus such as a piece of music is presented and children improvise in response to it. Although this is valuable experience it is also limited in its ability to permit aesthetic and creative growth and understanding. Sometimes prevailing concepts of creativity and expression in dance hinder the exploration of alternative dance experiences. Creativity is often regarded only in terms of the child discovering for him or herself movements which are original to him or her. The possibility of creative interpretation in performing or watching established dances for example is less frequently contemplated. Expression, too, can sometimes be taken to mean only self-expressive movement, the immediate response to a stimulus without the subsequent discipline of selecting, organising and structuring movement into a phrase or sequence, that is, a recognisable and repeatable expressive form. The concepts of creativity and expression in dance must be broadened and dance itself viewed in a wider context if its full potential as a means of aesthetic and creative education for children with a wide range of backgrounds, needs and abilities, is to be realised.

Occasionally folk and national dancing is included in the primary school curriculum, thereby providing additional and valuable dance experiences. However, the multicultural nature of our society should be more frequently acknowledged and the dances of ethnic minorities included alongside those of the indigenous population. As an integral part of the culture of many groups, dance is also an important and enjoyable means of promoting understanding among children from diverse backgrounds.

An added and unnecessary limitation on the effectiveness of dance experiences has been the conflation, in some cases, of content and method. Thus the teaching of folk dance has become associated with an exclusively direct approach, yet there is no reason why an established dance (or phrase or sequence) of any style should not be taught in an imaginative manner with opportunities for exploration and experimentation before specific steps and patterns are established. By the same token children devising their own dances are likely to benefit from occasional precise teacher intervention. This tendency to polarise teaching methods, associating certain approaches with particular types and styles of dance is not helpful, particularly when dealing with children with special needs. A teacher must always feel free to adopt those methods, techniques and strategies that are considered appropriate.

Developing aesthetic and creative understanding in dance

Aesthetic and creative understanding in dance can best be promoted by giving children opportunities to acquire a wide range of expressive movements, to compose and to appreciate dances. These types of experience should be made available from an early age, for as Howard Gardner (1973) the American psychologist has pointed out, the basis for the performer, the artist and the appreciator is already present in the very young child. Consequently, to omit any one of these would be to deny children access to a fully rounded dance education. This three-dimensional view of dance education also gives children opportunities to make progress aesthetically and creatively from a number of standpoints, an important consideration when there are children with individual special needs in a class. These are not however three distinct and separate aspects of dance; on the contrary they are inextricably linked and intertwined, experience in one area influencing and promoting understanding in another.

Nevertheless, distinguishing between them is a useful means of clarifying objectives for the teacher, for at any one time the major focus may be on extending the expressive movement range, the composition of dances or aesthetic appreciation.

Extending the range of expressive movement

Enlarging a child's repertoire of movements to enable the expression of various feelings and ideas is fundamental to dance teaching. The predominant means of achieving this objective in the nursery and primary school will be in the encouragement of individual imaginative responses to a range of visual and aural stimuli, but additional opportunities to learn, perform and watch dances of appropriate length and complexity will clearly help many children to increase their movement range.

The teacher must help each child to become aware of the body as an instrument of expression, not only as a complete unit but also in its constituent parts, including knees, elbows, fingers, toes and so on. A child should gradually realise that the body can travel in many different ways, but that stillness is also important; that surfaces of the body can lead movement in carving out pathways in space, making contrasting shapes and patterns; that steps and gestures can be executed initially to a steady beat, later to simple and ultimately complex rhythms. Most importantly, the time, tension and flow of movements can be varied and combined in numerous ways in order to change the expressive nature of the movement and therefore its meaning.

Increasing a movement vocabulary by encouraging individual imaginative responses to various stimuli enables each child to progress according to his own level of ability and understanding, in a relaxed non-competitive situation. The onus is on the teacher, however, to ensure that progress is in fact being made and that a child is indeed discovering new ways of moving expressively. While tasks should be sufficiently open-ended therefore to ensure that all children can be involved, limitations should also be clearly specified, for some children could very well be confused by excessive freedom and minimal direction.

Employing a variety of visual and aural aids is necessary if all children are to acquire a rich, well-rounded movement vocabulary. Contrasting types of stimuli are also likely to help gain and maintain the attention, interest and concentration of every child in the class. Consequently different types of music, percussive and vocal sounds, words, inanimate and animate objects, should be considered by the teacher. An additional advantage is that such stimuli are capable of providing the simple visual and aural images to which children of varying abilities can easily respond. The repeated presentation of a stimulus is also essential in order to give the child time to refine and then internalise an initial response.

An expressive movement vocabulary can also be increased by children learning a simple dance that comprises repetition of straightforward steps, gestures, rhythms and so on. Thus certain folk dances of the British Isles might be a useful and enjoyable means of learning specific step patterns; very different movement experience would be provided by participation in a dance based on Caribbean rhythms; learning Kathakali hand gestures would extend expressive movement skills in yet another way.

Watching dances is a further means of extending movement range, although dances must be carefully chosen to illustrate particular ways of moving. The power, strength and athleticism of the dancing in *Troy Games* for instance contrasts with the delicacy, sensitivity and ethereal movement representing that of ghosts and spirits in *Giselle*. In all cases, children's attention needs to be directed so that they notice the specific skills or qualities identified by the teacher and are not distracted by incidentals, for according to Gardner (1973) research shows that as early as nursery age, children are capable of attending to and absorbing qualitative aspects of art works, subsequently including such information in their own work.

Learning to make dances

In order to know how to make dances, it is important that all children are able to recognise a dance and so watching is a highly relevant experience in this instance too. A dance example might comprise a simple phrase, two or more phrases combined to form a sequence or a more complex arrangement that includes variation, contrast and repetition of steps, patterns and gestures. Such a dance could be an excerpt from a professional company's performance or one composed by children, but in each case, structure (how the parts of the dance are organised) and form (the overall appearance of the dance) will be clear and easily recognisable.

An alternative and important means of gaining knowledge and understanding of these key concepts of structure and form is by being part of a dance, for physical participation can give insights into the unique arrangement and organisation of movements that have been selected and combined to express a particular idea or feeling.

But perhaps the most valuable means of gaining knowledge and understanding relating to dance composition is for a child to be actually part of the creative process and therefore fully involved as creative agent in making dances of various types and styles. Such experience is often referred to as 'creative dance', beginning in the nursery school with the composition of simple movement phrases and culminating at the junior stage in the creation of dances characterised by varying degrees of complexity.

Children should be encouraged to use their own ideas for composing dances, but until they have the necessary experience and confidence in such creative work the teacher will most likely provide the initial idea. Even so, this will usually be in conjunction with pupils and arise either from their work in other areas of the curriculum or be related to their world beyond school, thereby making the whole experience as relevant and meaningful as possible. The alliance of dance with other creative arts means that many pieces of music, poems, nursery rhymes and stories explored in the classroom, as well as music, stories, poems, art, craft produced by the children themselves, will provide ideas for dance. Often the structure of one of these stimuli will be that of the dance too, for instance a simple AB or ABA arrangement or one with a chorus as in ABACAD ... and so on. The use of such established forms can also help clarify for children the meaning of structure and form in dance. Festivals such as Christmas, the Chinese Lantern Festival, Hallowe'en, provide excellent opportunities for exploration in dance and here the form will develop as the dance progresses.

Other areas of the curriculum, including religious studies, history, geography and science, may also suggest starting points. For instance the Schools Council's *On the Move* worksheets offer numerous possibilities, among them ideas relating to growth, communication and gravity. Incidentally, although the major purpose of dance experience is the development of creative and aesthetic understanding, valuable spin-offs may occur including the further clarification for some children of basic concepts that are also being explored in the classroom.

An important source of ideas lies in television. The latter is undoubtedly a highly significant part of the world of most children and this should be turned to advantage. Material that appeals to children, such as that involving puppets, robots, fantasy, can provide starting points by which imaginations can be stimulated and explorations made, so that pupils' own ideas and feelings about these stories and characters can be expressed in a dance form.

Developing dance appreciation

Appreciating a dance performance involves the recognition and enjoyment of the sensory qualities of the movement, that is the rhythms, skill, dynamics, flow, harmony and also the overall pleasing form of the dance. Involvement in the creative process of dance making and the experience of performing dances contribute substantially to growth in understanding and appreciation of dance as a whole. Occasional performances by children before an audience of other pupils, parents or friends are particularly valuable means of developing dance appreciation, for the dances must be thoroughly rehearsed and understood by the performers if expressive meanings are to emerge and be communicated to an audience.

The discipline necessary to achieve the appropriate standards and the pleasures gained from the enthusiastic response of an audience are additional and not inconsiderable benefits. There are some children who have few opportunities to shine publicly and the pride generated by being part of a successful performance is itself an emotion that all children should experience at some time. Such events can be highly significant occurrences in the lives of many children and so have enormous and lasting repercussions in terms of improved self-image and therefore general behaviour, attitudes and motivation.

In order to develop dance appreciation it is of fundamental importance that children also see good-quality dance performances by professional companies or others of equal standard, preferably in a theatre where the atmosphere can enhance the imaginative experience. The increasing availability of videotaped material, however, means that teachers everywhere can help children to become familiar with the work of the best dance companies in the world.

Dances must be well chosen in terms of length, subject matter and complexity, otherwise the experience could very well be a negative one. Ballet, modern dance, folk, national, ethnic and other dance companies are becoming more aware of the need to cater specifically for children by designing programmes especially for them. For instance a performance could include excerpts from certain classical ballets; *The Nutcracker* with its theme of dreams, toys and magic makes it especially suitable for young children. A more recent innovation has been the creation of dances especially for children of different ages, backgrounds and experience so that they can relate to and empathise with the work on stage. Even so, children need to be prepared for a performance, ideally by watching a videotape of the dances to be seen, but at least by being made familiar with any narrative content. Practical experience of some of the steps, patterns or phrases, is also likely to make the performance more meaningful to all the children in a class.

In recent years 'dance in education' companies and 'education units' attached to major companies have been formed, the main purpose being to work with children in their own school on all aspects of dance education, that is, performing, creating and appreciating. The style of dance offered, ballet, for instance, or an ethnic dance form, is often unfamiliar to the children and so these companies play an important rôle in extending and deepening dance awareness. The expertise that any highly trained dancer can bring should always be welcomed, but dancers are not necessarily educationalists and teachers should therefore work in partnership with them, ensuring that experiences are relevant and appropriate for all the children in the class, including any with special needs.

The involvement of dancers in schools is also valuable in providing concrete experiences that can enhance children's understanding of a dance performance on stage; practical experience of steps and patterns, handling shoes, headdresses and costumes are all useful. Important too, in the development of creative and aesthetic understanding, is the experience children are given of seeing the dancers they have actually met and talked to, transformed on stage into aesthetic images.

The presence of a dance company in a school can therefore help the teacher relate dance to a child's world, on the one hand making it more meaningful and, on the other, extending that world beyond the limitations imposed by a deprived environment or restricted lifestyle.

The dance programme

Most dance lessons in the primary school will be of a practical nature, although a short period spent watching a relevant videotaped dance extract could be very helpful in promoting learning. Such an extract could introduce a lesson illustrating the particular movement qualities or other objectives the teacher will subsequently be stressing. Alternatively an excerpt that is viewed at the end of a practical class could reinforce and consolidate learning that has taken place. The presentation of visual information in conjunction with kinaesthetic experience is a potent combination and a powerful means of encouraging children to learn, particularly those with learning difficulties.

Practical dance lessons begin with a brief warm-up period when the body is prepared physically for more vigorous demanding movement to follow. This introductory activity also sets the tone of the lesson, establishing expressive movement as the objective and not gymnastics or games. A substantial section is then devoted to the extension of a child's expressive movement range, the teacher selecting methods, techniques and stimuli in accordance with the needs of those in the class and the objectives of the lesson. Finally time is spent on producing and refining expressive forms, the visible evidence of the work of the creative imagination. The final products could be composed entirely by the child or the teacher, they could include established dances or emerge from a combination of these sources.

In the nursery and primary school the teacher's concern is progressively to extend and deepen a child's movement vocabulary for expressive purposes, in terms of awareness of the body, space, dynamics and rhythm. Increasingly complex combinations of these elements should be expected as knowledge and experience grow. The process of independently creating dances to express particular feelings and ideas begins initially by a child selecting movements to compose a simple phrase, followed by sequences and eventually fairly sophisticated forms. Children should gradually become more adept and sensitive performers, more skilful and more capable of expressing and communicating to others the emotions and ideas inherent in a dance. Growth in appreciation of different styles and types of dance should be evident in the ability to attend for progressively longer periods, noticing first of all the sensory and expressive characteristics and later with the benefit of maturity and experience basic aspects of structure and form. All of these dance experiences are inextricably intertwined, so that additional evidence of progress in any one area can often be ascertained by reference to the knowledge and understanding manifest in one of the others.

TEACHING CHILDREN WITH A WIDE RANGE OF NEEDS AND ABILITIES

Physical education and dance can make valuable contributions to the physical, emotional, social, cognitive, aesthetic and creative development of all children, whatever their needs. However, if each child in a class that includes a wide spectrum of abilities and backgrounds is to gain the greatest possible benefit from participation in gymnastics, games, swimming and dance, then lessons must be well structured with clear objectives and sound organisation, taking into account the various individual special needs of pupils. Throughout this chapter it has been stressed that teachers must be both positive and imaginative in their approaches, willing to reconsider established practices, methods and materials for instance, in order to maximise the learning capacity of every child. This final section focuses on the specific needs of the child with difficulties, for special consideration must be given to the provision of safe, secure teaching and learning environments so that the child can participate fully with others and be totally integrated into the class. For clarity of presentation this section is subdivided into the teacher–child relationship, safety, control and special needs in PE and dance, although there is obviously considerable overlap across these areas.

The teacher–child relationship

Most teachers recognise that a good relationship with a child is necessary for effective learning to take place. When the vulnerable child is involved, however, one who has met with persistent failure or who is withdrawn, disturbed or has other difficulties, then it is absolutely vital that the child likes and trusts the teacher. Confidence can be at a very low ebb and it is the teacher's task to restore self-respect; PE and dance situations, where the overall environment is very different from that of the classroom, can present ideal opportunities for a teacher to form a good relationship with a child. An observant teacher can also become aware of a difficulty during PE and dance lessons that has not come to light elsewhere; evidence of a potential physical or sensory impairment, for instance, or a problem with co-ordination. Sometimes a teacher, by merely recognising and accepting a difficulty, can greatly reduce a child's anxieties.

The relationship between a teacher and a child with special needs should perhaps be more accurately described as a partnership, with the teacher guiding the child through the learning process when necessary to ensure that success is experienced. Sometimes it is the acclaim of peers that a child requires to boost confidence and here a teacher can structure situations so that the necessary approval is received. Children with special needs tend to need praise and encouragement more frequently than most other children; advantages of PE and dance situations include the numerous opportunities that occur regularly when praise can be given and also recognised as genuine by the child concerned, which is of course a most important factor.

The teacher's own enthusiasm and positive attitude can be a key factor in developing not only confidence but also continuing interest in PE and dance. Active involvement, being a child's partner in a game for instance, or joining in a group sequence, can help cement all-important contacts between teacher and child. A warm and caring relationship with a child really is the key to satisfactory progress, optimising the opportunities available in PE and dance for fitness, recreation, aesthetic and creative enjoyment.

Safety

Safety in PE and dance lessons, a fundamental concern of every teacher, is highlighted when children with special needs are in the class. The special conditions pertaining to swimming have been referred to previously and control, obviously a major constituent of a safe environment, will be considered more fully in the next part of the section.

Teachers are often unduly fearful when working with children who have physical or sensory disabilities, yet if sensible precautions are taken there is no reason why they should not be fully integrated into the class. Lack of adequate information is the usual cause of excessive caution. A teacher needs to know exactly what limitations there are on physical involvement, the range and extent of the impairment, any medication prescribed and information on any particular ways of handling. No child should be put at risk, but on the other hand a child with a physical or sensory difficulty should be encouraged to lead as active a life as possible.

Full background information gives the teacher the confidence necessary to develop a child's independence and initiative, and to discourage over-protectiveness in others.

As far as the indoor physical environment is concerned, an important consideration for those who are clumsy or who have an impairment, is that the floor should be unpolished to reduce the possibility of slipping. Playgrounds should be smooth enough for a wheelchair or walking aid to be used without difficulty, although the child concerned must also be aware of natural hazards such as grids, sinks and so on; stones in grass can be another problem. When using a wheelchair or walking aid a child should be free to explore the space and not be confined to one area for 'safety'; other children in the class therefore need to be aware of their own responsibility in allowing the extra space and time a disabled child needs, but without isolating him. Similarly, children with limited sight and hearing often have poor spatial awareness and are therefore more likely to collide with others, so in this case too other children need to adapt their behaviour. Sensory impairments also demand the combined use of visual and aural stopping signals by the teacher, and as far as possible consistency in the placement and organisation of apparatus, membership of apparatus groups and so on to avoid any confusion. There are a number of opportunities during gymnastics and dance lessons when a wheelchair or walking aid could be discarded, with advantage to the child. Extra mats are likely to be needed and care should be taken that a child does not become overtired, although periodic rather than constant involvement in the lesson could overcome that problem.

Those with physical difficulties should be adequately clothed during PE lessons both indoors and outside. Movements are slower, the children become cold much more quickly than others and injuries could result. Clothing must, however, be suitable for physical activity: it must not interfere with movement nor should there be any danger of it catching on apparatus. This is particularly relevant to children from some cultural groups where there may be problems concerning the removal of jewellery or changing for PE. Bangles and other items worn by both sexes may be religious symbols, and from a very young age Muslim girls are usually required to cover their arms and legs when in mixed company. A teacher needs to be sensitive in explaining to parents the potential hazards of jewellery and flowing clothes during physical activity, particularly when apparatus is involved.

When children with behaviour difficulties are present, it is important that lessons are highly structured, well organised and progress smoothly without interruption. Physical environments should have as few distractions as possible; long curtains for instance should be tied back to reduce the temptation to hide behind them! Due consideration also needs to be given to the content of lessons; 'free-flow' or non-stop movement and certain types of accompaniment or stimuli can cause over-excitement and boisterous behaviour. Choice of equipment should also be taken into account, such as a soft ball in games, and the use of the hand rather than a bat may be a necessary precaution. In some instances in gymnastics it may even be wise to limit a child to certain pieces of apparatus that are known to cause least excitement. The teacher needs to keep close to a child with behaviour difficulties and maintain a calm disposition and voice at all times, otherwise the atmosphere, to which such children are particularly susceptible, can become increasingly tense, thereby exacerbating the situation. Sometimes it is helpful to hold and perhaps hug a child who is being particularly disruptive and a potential danger to others, until equanimity returns. In some dance situations, where the dangers are minimal because of the lack of equipment, it may be least disruptive to allow a hyperactive child to continue running around the room for part of the lesson. Other children in the class can very quickly become accustomed to this background 'noise' if attention is not drawn to it, thereby maintaining their own concentration. Teachers also report that while apparently not paying any attention, some hyperactive children are in fact absorbing information.

Control

Relaxed but effective control is fundamental not only for safety but also for successful teaching and learning. Many teachers, however, are intimidated by the PE and dance situations, fearing that difficulties encountered in the classroom will be increased when children are encouraged to move freely in large spaces, yet careful preparation and organisation can alleviate most problems.

Children with learning or behaviour difficulties respond to clear objectives, structured lessons and materials and established routines. Conversely problems can arise from a lack of clear direction in a lesson, for children need to know what they are supposed to be doing at all times, from the very start of the lesson. When PE and dance 'lessons' comprise little more than supervised play, then difficulties are almost certain to arise whether there are children with special needs in the class or not. Materials and teaching approaches can be selected in PE and dance so that all children are involved, working according to their own ability and experiencing success. A change in focus within a lesson can also help maintain attention, perhaps by means of variation in equipment, stimuli, activities and teaching approaches.

There should be established routines in every lesson. Arrangements for changing for PE and dance, moving between the classroom and hall or playground should follow prescribed patterns; there should be consistent visual and verbal stopping and starting signals that the children can recognise instantly and respond to accordingly. Bringing out and putting away apparatus or equipment provides potential opportunity for disruptive behaviour and it is therefore vital that organisation is efficient. Membership of groups should be maintained without change for as long as possible and those with behaviour difficulties placed with more mature children. Everyone should have the experience of working with a range of equipment during a lesson, but it is best if each group is given the responsibility of bringing out and putting away certain pieces of apparatus throughout any one term. If possible, apparatus should be placed around the hall (rather than in a cupboard) close to those areas where it will be used by the children, thereby avoiding unnecessary and lengthy carrying of equipment across a room with all the problems this can entail. If the playground or hall is over-large or of an awkward shape the space can be reorganised quickly using clearly recognisable, simple but stable markers so that close visual and aural contact can be maintained with potentially disruptive pupils. On the other hand children must be given adequate working space because, apart from the obvious physical dangers that could otherwise arise, pupils are more likely to interrupt and aggravate others if in constant close proximity to them. Dramatic weather, imminent festivals or special events can all cause extremes of behaviour and at these times a teacher needs to be particularly alert, selecting materials, planning and organising in accordance with this possibility.

Recognising the characteristics of a potentially disruptive situation and therefore defusing it quietly at an early stage without fuss and without drawing attention to the children concerned is a skill that a teacher must acquire. Simply leading an individual by the hand to a different part of the room as often as necessary while the lesson continues without interruption can be very effective. Placing an excitable child near to more mature members of the class can also be helpful. Whenever possible a child's work should be praised and when appropriate the child's own ideas employed, such as a suggestion for a dance or a game. This is possibly better than asking a child likely to present behaviour problems to demonstrate a skill or movement, as the opportunity to misbehave before a wide audience could prove irresistible and be a destructive experience for everyone concerned.

The teacher's aim should be to maintain a calm and secure working environment for all the children. However a teacher can inadvertently cause confusion and over-excitement by keeping up a constant monologue to no one in particular, as children explore apparatus for instance, or by competing with musical accompaniment in the mistaken belief that this will encourage more imaginative interpretations. Children should be allowed to concentrate on one thing at a time; indeed for many children this is in itself a difficult enough task. Teachers can use periods of general activity to observe the children, noting those who require help and taking the opportunity to give attention to those who need it. Long verbal explanations should also be avoided, whether addressed to the class as a whole or to particular children; short demonstrations and brief questions, comments and suggestions are more likely to be effective in maintaining the interest and concentration of everyone, especially when accompanied by praise and encouragement.

Special needs in PE and dance

In order to help all children to take full advantage of the potential offered by participation in PE and dance activities for integrated all-round development, a teacher must be aware of the particular needs of individual children. Such knowledge should be used to provide the conditions necessary for learning and to ensure that each child makes progress that is satisfying both to him or herself and the teacher. This knowledge however can be misused as, for example, when negative preconceptions of the child are formed. Research has frequently demonstrated that children fulfil expectations and consequently abilities often remain undeveloped because of lack of opportunity, a hostile environment or an unsympathetic teacher. A physical or sensory impairment, for example, may be viewed as an insurmountable problem rather than regarded in terms of the adaptations necessary on the part of the teacher and children in the class. Nor should it be assumed that a child experiencing specific difficulties in the classroom will automatically have similar problems in PE and dance. There is also the possibility that a child who is very capable in other areas of the curriculum may be clumsy and unco-ordinated in games and gymnastics lessons, causing great personal distress that could well be disregarded by a teacher who does not realise the possible implications for that child's social and emotional development. Teachers therefore not only need relevant background information but should also be alert and responsive to potential difficulties.

It has been pointed out earlier in the chapter that children with learning difficulties in the classroom can be very gifted physically in terms of agility, strength, co-ordination, grace of movement and skill. Sometimes, however, there can be problems relating to interpreting visual or verbal information, organising phrases or sequences, recognising relationships and employing simple tactics. Unless a teacher intervenes and helps develop understanding of basic rules and structures, then all-round progress in PE and dance will be limited.

When a child is unco-ordinated and clumsy it is vital that every opportunity is taken to increase his or her body awareness and help him or her acquire basic PE and dance skills during the early years. As well as breaking down material, providing realistic intermediate goals and therefore ensuring that success is a regular experience, time must be allowed for the practice and assimilation of skills. If there is the additional difficulty of limited concentration a teacher can help retain attention by the use of intrinsically interesting equipment and stimuli, by working in partnership with the child whenever possible and employing imaginative teaching methods.

Children with emotional problems can be found throughout the intellectual ability range, although the child with learning difficulties and the very gifted are known to be particularly vulnerable. Some children may need PE and dance experiences to release tensions and excess energies, to express feelings, emotions and conflicts. Other children are often very withdrawn and so the slightest physical effort must be praised, with the teacher persisting gently until full participation is realised. Experiences that incorporate moments of stillness and movements towards the centre of the body and away from it can be helpful in developing self-awareness and inner equilibrium. Children with emotional difficulties can have problems in establishing relationships with others; PE and dance situations are ideal means of assisting these children to make contact with others, a successful relationship in which the teacher is the first and crucial step.

Confidence, independence and perseverance are often very fragile qualities among children with special needs. Teacher anxieties can easily be conveyed to those with physical or sensory difficulties and so it is important that teachers are themselves confident in knowing as much as possible about each child's capabilities and limitations so that no one is put into a situation beyond their capabilities. Disabilities should be fully acknowledged as part of the child (with no inhibitions for instance in referring to an impairment) and so any necesssary modifications to tasks, apparatus arrangements, games and dance structures, should be the responsibility in the first instance of the teacher, but also that of other pupils so that integration can be authentic. Children with disabilities often need to be encouraged to persevere and teachers need to be firm as well as sympathetic in insisting that work is completed properly.

Children with hearing difficulties often try to hide their impairment and so teachers must be alert to this possibility. Percussion is a particularly appropriate accompaniment in dance as the vibration can be picked up more easily than other sounds; percussive sound therefore makes effective starting and stopping signals too.

The special needs of many children can be rooted in poor environmental conditions. Living in high-rise flats with inadequate play areas for instance can account for underdeveloped motor co-ordination, low levels of fitness and poor body awareness. Development can also be limited because of cultural traditions and in some cases religious rules. Play learning activities may have low priority in homes that are highly disciplined, and imaginative, creative work may not be highly regarded. Parents, keen on academic success may not realise the value of PE activities in terms of all-round integrated development; playing games, for instance, may be seen as having little educational value with the result that children are not encouraged to develop gifts. Teachers must therefore be prepared to explain the importance of participation in PE and dance. Teacher awareness of the traditional sporting preferences and abilities of different groups can also be helpful in involving all children and promoting understanding. Advantage can also be taken of the place dance has in the culture of many ethnic communities, where it is often linked closely with religion or is an integral part of celebrations. Many opportunities arise therefore for the teacher to involve parents and other members of the local community in providing enriching experiences for all.

Monitoring progress in PE and dance

Throughout this chapter it has been stressed that all children can achieve success and make satisfactory progress in PE and dance. Indications have also been given of broad stages of development in gymnastics, games, swimming and dance, against which individual progress may be judged. PE and dance lessons can also provide an observant teacher with clear indicators of a child's physical, emotional, social, aesthetic and creative growth.

Improved physical development can be seen in a child who is more alert and whose endurance, fitness, agility, flexibility, mobility and co-ordination have increased. Evidence of a child's satisfactory social development may be found in greater involvement and co-operation with other children in sharing equipment and taking turns; sometimes the positive attitudes of other children are signs of social integration. Healthy emotional growth is often first indicated by improved posture, for as self-image improves an upright stance develops replacing the 'hang-dog' look so often found among children who have emotional or learning difficulties. As confidence increases, so too does independence and with it self-discipline. Improved cognitive functioning may be shown in PE and dance in the ability to concentrate for progressively longer periods, making appropriate responses to tasks set by the teacher and employing discrimination and selection in the construction of sequences, games and dances. Aesthetic development is shown in a child's grace, sensitivity and harmony of movement; in awareness of shape, line and rhythm in personal work and that of others; in general interest in and enthusiasm for various sports and dance. Indicators of creative understanding include the individual nature of responses, imaginative structuring of phrases and sequences, novel ideas for games and dances and creative interpretations of dances in performance and as a spectator.

Whenever circumstances permit, children should experience all aspects of PE and dance for each contributes in specific and unique ways to a child's overall development.

REFERENCES AND RESOURCES

Local Education Authorities usually offer some practical assistance, such as an ancillary worker, to teachers who have children with special needs in their classes. In-service courses are also often available, while additional support and advice can generally be obtained from the PE adviser.

Many LEAs now publish their own PE and dance curriculum literature, some of which is related specifically to children with special needs. For example, *Lancashire looks at ... Physical Education in the Special School* (1985) published by Lancashire County Council and *Physical Education and Physically Handicapped Pupils in Day Schools* (n.d.) published by Kent County Council.

Other curriculum literature that is readily available includes:

Groves, L. (ed.) (1979) *Physical Education for Special Needs*. Cambridge: Cambridge University Press.

Levete, G. (1982) *No Handicap to Dance*. London: Souvenir Press.

Price, R.J. (1980) *Physical Education and the Physically Handicapped*. London: Lepus Books.

Upton, G. (ed.) (1979) *Physical and Creative Activities for the Mentally Handicapped*. Cambridge: Cambridge University Press.

The following are not concerned specifically with special needs but contain relevant material:

Boorman, J. (1973) *Dance and Language Experiences with Children*. Ontario: Longman.

Joyce, M. (1984) *Dance Technique for Children*. California: Mayfield.

Shreeves, R. (1979) *Children Dancing*. London: Ward Lock Educational.

Articles on the curriculum may be found in the *Journal of the Physical Education Association* and *Drama and Dance*.

The achievements of those with special needs can be an inspiration to all teachers and children; lists of videotapes and films available for hire can be found in LEA and other literature given above. There are also numerous flourishing national and local associations concerned with sport for the disabled where the teacher can seek additional advice and information. A predominant aim, however, should be to integrate children with special needs into the local community and so contacts should be made with officials of local community organisations, sports clubs, Cubs, Brownies, leisure centres, swimming baths, dance groups, to discover what facilities and arrangements there are for those with special needs. Addresses of the various local and national groups referred to can usually be obtained from libraries. The following organisations are also able to provide useful information:

Physical Education Association of Great Britain and Northern Ireland, Ling House, 162 Kings Cross Road, London WC1X 9DH.

The Central Council for Physical Recreation, Francis House, Francis Street, London SW1P 1DG.

For information relating to dance companies working in schools contact the Education Unit, The Arts Council, Piccadilly, London W1. Regional Arts Associations can also be helpful.

There is a growing research literature on the relationships between movement experiences and those with special needs. The following are a representative sample of established influential texts:

Cratty, B.J. (1974) *Motor Activity and the Education of Retardates*. Philadelphia: Lea and Febiger.

Frostig, M. and Maslow, P. (1973) *Learning Problems in the Classroom*. New York: Grune and Stratton.

Kephart, N.C. (1960) *The Slow Learner in the Classroom*. Columbus, Ohio: Charles Merrill.

Moran, J.M. and Kalakian, L.H. (1978) *Movement Experiences for the Mentally Retarded and Emotionally Disturbed Child*. Minneapolis: Burgess.

Morris, P.R. and Whiting, H.T.A. (1971) *Motor Impairment and Compensatory Education*. London: Bell.

Details of the relationship between motor development and environmental factors may be obtained by reference to:

Cherrington, D. (1980) *Leverhulme Research Project: Environmental and Motor Deprivation*. Centre of Advisory Studies of Education, University of Birmingham.

For information about research into primary children's physical activity outside school, consult:

Dickinson, B. (1986) The physical activity patterns of young people – the implications for physical education. *Bulletin of Physical Education*, **22**, 36–39.

or contact: N. Armstrong, School of Education, University of Exeter.

Publications concerned specifically with art and aesthetic development include:

Gardner, H. (1973) *The Arts and Human Development*. New York: Wiley.

Redfern, B. (1986) *Questions in Aesthetic Education*. London: Allen and Unwin.

Ross, M. (1982) *The Development of Aesthetic Experience*. Oxford: Pergamon Press.

Whiting, H. T. A. and Masterson, D. W. (eds) (1974) *Readings in the Aesthetics of Sport*. London: Lepus.

Journals reporting recent research into various aspects of physical education and dance include the *Bulletin of Physical Education*, the *Physical Education Review* and *The Journal of Aesthetic Education*.

—4—

Music

Jean Turnbull

'Music should be an integral part of every child's daily experience.'
This is a laudable statement from Her Majesty's Inspectors'
publication *Music from 5 to 16* (DES, 1985). Although they have
limited this to children in nursery, infant and lower junior schools, it
is even more essential that it is applied to children with special
needs since it is one subject area that allows communication, both
verbal and non-verbal, and can accommodate children with a wide
range of different abilities in a shared and worthwhile experience.
All children should be encouraged to listen to, participate in and
enjoy music of all kinds and it should be possible within a
well-structured music curriculum to cater for the needs of all
children regardless of age or ability.

As Music Co-ordinator for the Brent Education Authority, I have
been fortunate to work alongside caring and talented staff in
promoting a programme of musical integration with children from
both mainstream and special schools. We have worked positively
towards encouraging children of all ages to work together, initially
in one group, but, after two years, we have now been able to set up
workshops where children from similiar age groups, infants,
juniors and seniors, work with their peers making and exploring
both music and movement. This approach has proved very
successful since it has shown both to the teaching staff and the older
children in secondary schools that pupils with special needs are
equally if not more able to make music of a very high standard. By
making a careful choice of music that allows children to contribute at
the level of their ability, these workshops have proved that there are
few boundaries to introducing all children to this shared and
worthwhile experience.

There are many books that outline the teaching of class music and
an endless selection of music books for children, but the area that is
less well-documented is how and what to use with children who
have special needs. Whether chair-bound or ambulant, these
children may be unable to benefit from the music lesson unless the

teacher understands their individual requirements and recognises that some adjustments to his or her teaching methods may be necessary in order to accommodate certain types of disability. In the course of this chapter, I intend to examine the practical factors that must be considered when teaching musical skills to children who may have little or no experience of music, or may previously have been educated in special schools.

Music encompasses all classes of basic skills: aural; visual; linguistic; motor; and social; and it is perhaps interesting to equate them with the areas of difficulty experienced by some of the children now being educated in mainstream schools. The profoundly deaf or partially-hearing child will require extra help in acquiring aural skills. For the child with visual impairment, the acquisition of visual skills will be very difficult. For the child with learning difficulties, problems with language and speech are frequently the most common source of difficulty, while children with physical disabilities may have seriously impaired motor skills. Finally, social skills are often noticeably absent from children who present behavioural problems. This is a simplistic analogy but it may provide a basis for elementary assessment for the teacher faced with certain kinds of special needs.

AURAL AWARENESS

Aural awareness can be encouraged in all children from an early age by the sensible choice of simple songs, singing games, action songs and movement to music. Listening to and recognising environmental sounds and distinguishing between sound and silence all assist in developing early listening skills. It is always important to be aware of the difference between hearing and listening however, since the latter requires an intellectual response. Most children will hear what is said to them but will often not respond to the instruction that is given as they have failed to intellectualise and evaluate what has been asked of them. 'Listen' is probably the most overused word in any teacher's vocabulary since many children seldom listen to instructions, which have often to be repeated.

It is frequently assumed that the person with visual difficulties will be 'good at music'. This assumption is based on the premise that the aural sense compensates for poor vision and that heightened aural awareness is synonymous with musicality. I can speak only from my own experience with partially-sighted children but I did not find this to be the case initially. These children are undoubtedly responsive to sound, but in musical terms they can be as unaware as other children and it is important that they learn to distinguish conscious listening from hearing. Once the child makes this distinction, he or she can develop musical skills to a very high level. Singing is the most obvious way of encouraging good aural perception and, since there is usually no speech impairment attached to visual disability, it is the most accessible form of music making for partially-sighted children.

Over a period of time it is possible to train young children to sing in parts, make up their own harmonies and improvise successfully and the partially-sighted child will soon become very adept at spotting defects in intonation. Since visual skills present problems, there is little value in issuing songbooks even with large print as they will only obscure the mouths of the readers and reduce the volume and quality of sound. The children then rely completely on the teacher for the words of the songs. It is important to remember that most partially-sighted children have never seen a page of words, a paragraph or perhaps even a sentence since their reading world tends to consist of one word or one letter at a time. They will learn mostly by rote, which makes the teacher's rôle particularly important in pronouncing the words of songs as clearly as possible. Partially-sighted children will often make a song sound very intense since, by misplacing accents, they give equal stress to the unimportant as well as to the important syllables of words within sentences. This highlights again the need for conscious listening on the part of the child and for good clear diction on the part of the teacher.

VISUAL AWARENESS

The understanding of music relies substantially on the understanding of musical concepts and although music should be primarily an aural experience, the fact that it is notated will also require the development of visual skills at some stage. Certain musical concepts are learned more easily by the use of visual material and since a considerable amount of early learning is visual, the music lesson must also include the development of visual awareness.

For the child who is partially-sighted or registered blind, this skill will be difficult or impossible to acquire but for hearing-impaired children, visual stimuli are particularly important. My own experience in this area confirms that when using written solfa in conjunction with solfa hand signs, both profoundly deaf and partially-hearing children display a well-developed visual memory and are very receptive to pitch directions taught in this way. By using either the Kodaly scheme as translated in Cecilia Vajda's book

The Kodaly Way to Music (1974) or by incorporating the New Curwen Method of solfa, which is an updated and more modern version of that of the founder of solfa, John Curwen, it is possible to assist the hearing-impaired child to assimilate several different musical concepts. Register and direction are two of the most useful concepts to teach children with a hearing loss since one of the most obvious factors to a hearing person working with hearing-impaired children is the apparent lack of speech inflection in their voices. By using two different pitches such as *soh*, the higher sound, and *doh*, the lower sound, and by signing them, children can be taught to stress the important syllable in a word by using the higher sound and to put less stress on the weaker syllable by using the lower sound. For example, *to put less stress on the weaker syllable* would translate in solfa terms as *d d d d d d s d d d* with the strong accent falling on the syllable 'weak'. Rhythmic patterns are also important in relation to words and again by using visual material such as a flannelgraph board children can learn simple rhythmic notation, firstly by using words and visual symbols such as *cat and kittens* and when these are known, replacing them with standard notation, that is, crotchets and quavers, and by giving them French time names, *ta* and *ta te*. Similar examples appear in the Kodaly Method.

A considerable amount of research has been done over the years into music and the hearing-impaired. The success of Evelyn Glennie, the Scottish percussionist who won the Shell Music Scholarship after studying at the Royal Academy of Music, has given encouragement both to music educators and to other hearing-impaired people. Claus Bang, a Danish music therapist, has worked for many years using large bass resonator bars to assist in training children with hearing problems to sing and speak. These bars span a range of 64–380 Hz and with this pitch range, they stimulate residual hearing among hearing-impaired students. Bang describes his work as musical speech therapy and states that the 'method provides one of the best-known means to improve the voice material of hearing-impaired persons and their ability to perceive and reproduce the inflections of speech resulting in an increased intelligibility and improved communication'.

For most children, visual material will assist in developing certain musical concepts, in particular, register and direction. The *Silver Burdett Music Scheme*, published in America but used in many parts of this country, produce a chart book for young children as part of the scheme in which pictures have been specially chosen to encourage visual awareness and to help to promote the understanding of musical concepts.

Pitched percussion instruments such as chime bars, glockenspiels, xylophones and metallophones are also invaluable as both aural and visual resources because they will provide an aid to such concepts as register, tone-colour, harmony and direction and although an expensive addition to this collection, Sonor bass bars help to develop recognition of low pitched sounds. It makes it easier for young children if these instruments are placed in an upright position because it reinforces visually, both register and direction. In this position they demonstrate that the bigger the bar, the lower the sound, a fact which is not so easily determinable when the instruments are placed horizontally. By incorporating these instruments for the accompaniments of songs, young children can learn to play short, stepwise patterns that may occur as part of a song, or add an octave ostinato throughout a song, thus helping again to develop awareness of register, tempo and dynamics as well as other factors that make for the understanding of music. From this stage, it is a short step towards simple notation. Children already possess the treble and bass staves on each hand and can learn to work out the letters of the treble stave on the fingers of one hand. Once children understand simple concepts, they can then develop more advanced skills by making up their own compositions, notating scores either by traditional methods or by using their own form of graphic notation.

LANGUAGE SKILLS

Music is often erroneously described as being a 'universal language', possibly on the assumption that it is to be found throughout the world, but the way in which music is practised in certain countries will not mean or convey the same as in other countries. Nevertheless, in most cases, it does require the acquisition of language and in many cases the acquisition of language is facilitated through singing. Singing, and particularly encouragement to sing well unaccompanied, should be every child's introduction to the world of music. Every culture has its own heritage of simple songs or nursery rhymes and some are common to a variety of cultures. I have found several versions of *Twinkle, Twinkle Little Star*, one of them in Armenian, and regardless of the number of other infant songs I have taught, this is invariably the one that is most often requested by children from a wide variety of nationalities.

Language programmes receive a high priority in schools for young children and they are also essential in teaching children with learning difficulties, particularly children who are unable to read or for children whose first language is not English. As with hearing and listening in relation to aural skills and seeing and looking in relation to visual skills, it is important to distinguish between language and speech, or what is said and how it is said. Again it is the use of songs that will facilitate this distinction. Carefully chosen songs with simple words, with words that are constantly repeated; echo songs, or songs that require the words to be remembered in the correct sequence, will assist in the learning of language and help to build up an understanding of the spoken word.

Children who have very limited language skills will benefit from a well-structured and well chosen programme of songs. These songs might include the use of the response to their own names, giving simple instructions for actions or for finding objects or asking and expecting a reply to a simple question. Songs can also assist in developing body awareness, learning concepts, perceptual skills, identification of colour and a certain degree of numeracy. The music therapy programme established by the Americans Nordoff and Robbins contains many songs of this kind. Music therapy is now recognised as a specific treatment for learning disorders and the Nordoff–Robbins technique is one of several now used in this country. It is based on the response of children to many different styles of music. The work has been developed principally with children with severe learning problems. The results of this work have been collated and are used to provide the basis for a music therapy treatment that has been found to be successful with autistic children and children with hearing problems as well as those with profound learning difficulties.

The Dartington project set up by Professor Jack Dobbs and the Standing Conference for Amateur Music in 1968 subsequently published several booklets under the title *Music for Slow Learners* (Dobbs). Included in these booklets are many illuminating ideas on how to assist speech and improve language skills. Doctor Audrey Wisbey in conjunction with the British Broadcasting Corporation has produced a book based on her own experiences with children with learning problems entitled *Learn to Sing to Learn to Read* (1982). In recent years, book publishers have become more aware of the need to provide simple, good quality material and several publications are now on the market, some of which have been provided by teachers who are working with children who have special needs and for whom they have written the material.

MOTOR SKILLS

It is neither easy, nor necessarily relevant, to say which skill music influences most, but in the development of motor skills, the playing of instruments, movement to music and action songs will certainly have a considerable contribution to make. Children with a physical disability are probably the principal group who experience difficulty in learning motor control since their disability may affect the use of one or more of their limbs. This is most noticeable in children who are cerebral-palsied. Spasticity can affect one side of the body (hemiplegia), the lower limbs (paraplegia) or all four limbs (quadraplegia). Where damage to the brain is mild, the cerebral palsied child will cope relatively well with practical music making. Brass instruments such as the French horn are ideal for a child who has right-sided hemiplegia. String instruments and the more recent addition of electronic instruments are equally suited to this child. The more severely disabled child, who is often non-ambulant, has problems with balance and a musical instrument that demands a large arm movement in order to play it will often result in spasm of the limbs. It is here that adaptations of classroom instruments are often necessary. This type of adaptation has been well-documented in Philip Bailey's excellent book *They Can Make Music* (1973) and in the American publication *Clinically Adapted Instruments for the Multiply Handicapped* (Clark and Chadwick, 1980).

The child suffering from cerebral palsy may, as a result of damage to the brain, also experience perceptual problems and related learning difficulties whenever expected to cross the 'mid-line'. This is a somewhat vague term for a point around the middle of the body over which the child normally learns to transfer in his or her early stages of development. The mid-line syndrome will often make the cerebral palsied child appear clumsy, particularly when playing an instrument that requires movement from left to right or the reverse. Similarly, when reading elementary music notation such as *Middle C, D, Middle C*, this child may be unable to relate the first note to the third since this involves transference across the mid-line. For the latter, flash cards and mnemonics will assist in the assimilation of music notation.

The athetoid child who finds purposeful movement difficult will consequently find the handling of musical instruments something of a problem and any activity demanding precise rhythmic control will accentuate the involuntary movement associated with this condition. A teacher may find it helpful to seek advice from physiotherapists. A splint for example, can be made for the child's arm and he or she will then be able to contribute sound effects on any large instrument requiring the use of a beater. The athetoid child has fewer perceptual problems and although speech impairments are often quite severe, this child may be intellectually very aware and will appreciate sensible and worthwhile musical tasks.

The ataxic child who has problems with balance also experiences difficulty when holding a musical instrument. Once more, precise use of pitched or non-pitched instruments makes unnecessary demands on a child with this condition. In my own experience, I have found that ataxic children possess a better fine finger than gross motor control and appear more at ease with small keyboard instruments such as Melodicas or electronic keyboards. Again, it is the responsibility of the teacher to find out with which instrument the child feels most comfortable. One important point that may be added to this is that music should be made for music's sake. Where the damage to the limbs of children is irreversible, it is better for the music teacher to promote a feeling of enjoyment and a sense of musical achievement than to seek to encourage instrumental playing as a form of therapeutic exercise.

Children with spina bifida often have little or no sensation below the waist. An analogy I was given was to an egg in an egg cup. It is therefore necessary to realise that when positioning such a child for a musical activity, he or she has little sense of balance in the lower half of the body and balance is achieved by using the arms for support. This will mean that when children wish to play a two-handed instrument such as a recorder or glockenspiel, they will require a desk or table on which to balance themselves.

One further area of concern when dealing with young people who experience problems with motor skills are the group who suffer from muscular dystrophy. Muscular dystrophy is a wasting of the muscles through fat taking the place of protein. It is an upsetting condition in terms of physical deterioration and it is reflected within the music lesson in that these children are progressively less able to play certain musical instruments and may find sustained singing becomes more difficult. Initially, a young child in an infant school will be able to cope with the class music lesson as well as his or her peer group. As these children grow older, however, and the muscles become weaker, they are less able to play instruments that demand any real physical effort. Gradually, as the condition worsens, they may be capable of only a very limited finger movement or may require to use a prosthesis in order to play an instrument. The use of electronic keyboards will help these young children to participate in the music lesson as well as instruments such as the ethnic talking drums wherein a wide variety of pitches may be obtained with a very limited wrist movement. A sensitive teacher will realise how much a child is physically capable of and will make appropriate musical allowances so that he or she can work at the level of the disability. It is important to remember that children with muscular dystrophy expend considerable mental effort in coping with their physical condition so that at times it may appear as if they are not really concentrating on a specific task but they achieve immense satisfaction in accomplishing musical objectives and should always be encouraged to take part.

Singing lessons are always an enjoyable experience when working with children who have a physical disability, even though some conditions like athetosis do affect speech. Young children can be assisted through the use of songs to improve perceptual functioning, develop learning concepts and achieve a better degree of motor skill. If it is possible to obtain the assistance of a number of adults from both teaching and paramedical staff, young children can be given guidance with the actions for songs, which will help to direct the learning of body awareness, encourage movement and reinforce simple concepts.

Whenever practical music making takes place, posture is of paramount importance. Whether it is choral, orchestral or class-room music making, the correct way of standing or sitting is rudimentary but essential. It is doubly important when dealing with children who have special needs. It is well worth-while to take advice from physiotherapists or occupational therapists who may already be working with these children, but, if there is no paramedical person to consult, always ask the child in which position he or she is most comfortable as this will assist children to reach their full potential from the music lesson.

SOCIAL SKILLS

Children who are emotionally insecure or socially disadvantaged will often find that music, whether through a passive or active involvement, can provide both an emotional and social enrichment to their lives. Most children are subjected to or opt for a wide variety of popular music, but many children who are emotionally disturbed may sometimes find that within the more intellectual requirements of classical music, there is something in the melody, rhythm, harmony or tone-colour that has an immediate appeal. When this is the case, they should be encouraged to listen to more of the same or to more advanced music. Often, this is a pursuit that they follow without guidance, but if they can be persuaded to bring this interest into the classroom and share it with their teacher and classmates, it may help to establish a better behaviour pattern and give these children more confidence in themselves. In the process of exposing children to a wide range of music, the teacher may notice some surprising responses from children who do not usually show much enthusiasm for other areas of the school curriculum. The variety of music chosen for listening should encompass serious art forms, traditional music of many cultures and popular music of the present day. It is essential that an initial simple listening programme is devised so that the children are made aware of this wide diversity and are encouraged to explore the nature of sound and the meaning of music.

The music syllabus for the General Certificate of Secondary Education requires candidates to listen, perform and compose and it should be within the scope of a good primary teacher with responsibility for music to incorporate these three areas into a similar programme for young children. This would be of particular benefit to children with special needs. If positively directed, listening to music should demand both conscious listening and a fair degree of concentration, both of which can be somewhat lacking in children who have learning difficulties. By playing short extracts of different music, teachers may discover how the children react to music. Do they like or dislike it; what associations does it evoke; what elements does it contain in relation to musical concepts such as timbre, texture, melody, rhythm, harmony, register or dynamics? If the music contains a simple pitch or rhythmic structure or a repetitive figure, is it possible to reproduce this vocally or on a classroom instrument? For example, if a work such as Beethoven's *Symphony No 7 in A (Op. 92)* was used, the repetitive rhythm of the allegretto movement is easily followed using non-pitched percussion to accompany the short pattern ♪♫ | ♫♪ | ♪♫ | ♪ . A more advanced rhythmic pattern is present in *Bolero* by Ravel and there are many other examples, particularly within the popular idiom, that can be used to illustrate rhythm patterns and rhythmic ostinati.

Listening to music that contains simple harmonic structures can become a practical lesson in pitch. Pachelbel's *Canon in D* contains four melodic lines each of which children can reproduce vocally from the very simple to the more complex. By using solfa symbols or a simple vowel sound, the children do not need to verbalise but can produce a satisfactory musical result within a relatively short time. The easiest line contains two sounds, *soh* and *lah* (*s s l s l s l s*) Two other lines contain stepwise progressions: *d' t l s f m f r* and *m' r' d' t l s l t* while the final line provides the basis of the harmony: *d' s l m f d f s*. These lines can also be played on pitched percussion instruments. By performing this piece, children will gain experience of melody, harmony, tempo, direction and dynamics. A study of the music of Africa shows that in several African countries a considerable number of *call and response* songs exist in which the response is often sung to a single vowel sound or to a group of different vowel sounds. For children with limited speech or for those who cannot cope with the lengthier verses of some traditional songs, both the repetition and the simplicity of the response can encourage a real sense of participation. The rhythmic qualities of African music are also stimulating and exciting in themselves and produce a reaction from most children.

By adopting a musical programme that involves listening, playing and singing, children develop musical skills and by acquiring these skills, will gradually gain confidence in their own ability to make music. For the child who is emotionally insecure or socially disadvantaged, these forms of music making will help to encourage social awareness. Where children are involved in practical music making, particularly when a performance is the end product, it is important for them to recognise that their rôle is essential to the overall result and that each child must be responsible for his or her own part within the group. Given this responsibility, most children do measure up to the challenge and do learn that there is enormous satisfaction to be gained from doing something well.

Although there are a considerable number of books on music, song books and other musical material, it is perhaps worth directing teachers of music, particularly in primary schools, towards publications that have been specifically written for children with special needs. Probably the most carefully researched work in this field is that of the American writers Nordoff and Robbins, whose work with children with severe learning difficulties, and, latterly, Robbins' work with hearing-impaired children, has resulted in several books on the subject as well as several collections of songs. Over the years in which Nordoff and Robbins worked with these children, they documented their work in some detail. This documentation finally emerged as a 'treatment' for various learning difficulties and resulted in the setting up of the Nordoff–Robbins Centre for Music Therapy. Many local education and health authorities have appreciated the advantages of recruiting music therapists to work in both schools and hospitals and the field has increased considerably over the last decade. For a more practical use of their material in mainstream schools, Nordoff and Robbins have published a series of *Children's Playsongs*, which assist very young children to learn simple concepts such as colour, days of the week, numbers and the names of children in their class. The songs are simple although the musical idiom is more complex and the piano accompaniments demand a fairly high degree of expertise from the teacher. Most of the songs were inspired by the children with whom they were working and the authors state that 'it is important to preserve the element of play'. All these songs work equally well with children in infant schools, as well as with those for whom they were designed.

Music therapy is now well-established in this country and many courses are run in various music departments, universities and centres. Much of the success that has been achieved was the result of the pioneering work of Juliette Alvin who has written several books on the subject that would be of interest to both specialists and non-specialists (Alvin, 1976, 1978, 1983). Music therapy has been described as 'the controlled use of music in a physiological or psychological treatment. Music is used as a therapeutic means in a clinical situation'. The specialist nature of this training means that therapy of this kind should only be practiced by someone who is fully qualified but many of the ideas and songs contained in specialist books are equally applicable to all young children.

Two music educators have also contributed much to the literature of music for special needs. David Ward has worked extensively with young people and is Principal Officer of the Dartington Music Foundation for the Handicapped. His books *Hearts and Hands and Voices* (1976) and *Sing a Rainbow* (1979) show a sensitive and caring response to the musical needs of children as well as providing expert advice to teachers working in music with children of all ages. Two smaller booklets based on the Slow Learners Project initiated by the Standing Conference for Amateur Music have equally useful information for teaching singing and for organising sound activities. The bibliography and appendices require updating but much of the information is still valid.

Jan Holdstock's impressive collection of short musical plays and songs should be in every infant, junior and special school's music library. Their delightful titles, for example *Hannibal the Cannibal* (1979c) and *Eggosaurus Box!* (1979b), contain many excellent ideas for both musical and non-musical activities.

Perhaps an activity for which the Master of the Queen's Music, Malcolm Williamson, is less well-known is the work that he does with young people and adults with learning difficulties. I have had the pleasure of seeing him work with a large number of young children from London who prepared and performed one of his 'cassations', *The Snow Wolf* (1970). He has published eight works under this heading, which he describes as 'tiny operas to be performed in schoolrooms, in the open air or anywhere informal'. He states that there should be no audience and 'since there is no audience to judge the performance, polished perfection is less important than abandon and enjoyment'. *The Snow Wolf* is a particularly felicitous work since it functions on different musical and linguistic levels. There are four singing groups involved, one of which is a train. Throughout the work, it is possible for this group to sing only the words *chuff a chuff*, which is ideal for children with limited language skills.

At least two American publications exist that are both useful as a music resource. One is the unfortunately named *Music Activities for Retarded Children* (Ginglend and Stiles, 1981). This is a ring-bound book of some one hundred pages containing finger play and action songs, folk dances and other related musical activities and would be of use with children of infant and junior school age. The second is a series of publications forming a music course that spans the age range from infant to third-year secondary school. This is called *Silver Burdett Music* and although some of the terminology is not in common use in this country, the material has been carefully selected and impeccably presented. Each of the levels is self-contained and can be used separately or as part of the complete scheme. In each book, there are suggestions to teachers on the adaptation of the material to suit children with disabilities as well as a separate book *Reaching the Special Learner through Music*. Although the musical material, which is also backed by recordings, is expensive, there is little other material available that has been so comprehensively put together and well-illustrated.

The Music Advisory Service of the Disabled Living Foundation has been available for some years and its range of advice has grown considerably through the publication of resource papers that cover almost every aspect of music and disablement. There are 21 papers, which include such information as music for the partially-sighted, music for the hearing impaired, music books for nursery children and music books related to disabled people. A twice-yearly news letter, *Music News* is available free of charge and provides information on recent developments and advice on all areas connected with music and disability. For any parent, musician, teacher or student, this advisory service is quite invaluable.

Music will evoke different responses from different people, but whether they are listening to music or performing, it is capable of providing emotional, intellectual and physical involvement to a very high degree. Music teachers must make it a subject that is accessible and enjoyable, but above all must ensure that they foster in their pupils a sense of self-esteem. This is paramount when working with children who are already disadvantaged by a particular handicap. The professional music world contains many personalities who have overcome severe disabilities and reached the height of the profession. It is therefore important for teachers to realise that they may have within their care, a future Itzhak Perlman, Stevie Wonder, Geoffrey Tate or Ian Dury who, because of their disabilities, might easily have been overlooked within the education system. It should be a priority for every music teacher to plan their teaching in a way that allows every child to respond to music at his or her own level and for the teacher to be aware of any small talent or interest in their subject that may be encouraged and allowed to reach full fruition.

SUGGESTED BIBLIOGRAPHY

Song books for primary schools

Birch, B. (ed.) (1985) *Assemblies Around the Year*. London: Ward Lock Educational.

Bird, W. and McAuliffe, G. (eds) (1978, 1979) *Sing a Song* Books 1 and 2. London: Nelson.

Brandling, R. (ed.) (1983) *Every Colour under the Sun: A Collection of Songs for Primary School Assemblies*. London: Ward Lock Educational.

Conolly, Y. (ed.) *Mango Spice: 44 Caribbean Songs*. London: A. & C. Black.

Diamond, E. (rev. ed. 1987) *Act One, Sing Too*. London: Chappell.

Gadsby, D. and Golby, I. (eds) (1978) *Merrily to Bethlehem: A Very Unusual Carol Book*. London: A. & C. Black.

Gadsby, D. and Harrop, B. (eds) (1982) *Flying a Round: 88 Rounds and Partner Songs*. London: A. & C. Black.

Gilbert, J. (1980) *Topic Anthologies*: 1: *Transport*; 2: *Circuses and Fairs*; 3: *Cowboys and Indians*; 4: *Festivals*. Oxford: Oxford University Press.

Gray, V. (1975) *Knives and Forks and Spoons*. Potton, Beds: Lindsay Music.

Gray, V. (1980) *Apple Pie and Custard*. Potton, Beds: Lindsay Music.

Harrop, B. (ed.) (1973) *Carol, Gaily Carol: Christmas Songs for Children*. London: A. & C. Black.

Harrop, B. (ed.) (1975) *Apusskidu*. London: A. & C. Black.

Harrop, B. (ed.) (1976) *Okki-Tokki-Unga: Action Songs for Children*. London: A. & C. Black.

Harrop, B. (ed.) (1983) *Sing Hey Diddle Diddle: 66 Nursery Rhymes with Their Traditional Tunes*. London: A. & C. Black.

Holdstock, J. (1979a) *Colours of Christmas*. London: Universal Edition.

Holdstock, J. (1979b) *Eggosaurus Box!* London: Universal Edition.

Holdstock, J. (1979c; new ed. in preparation) *Hannibal the Cannibal*. London: Universal Edition.

Holdstock, J. (1980) *Turnip Head*. London: Universal Edition.

Holdstock, J. (1981a) *The Christmas Dragon*. London: Universal Edition.

Holdstock, J. (1981b) *The Ginger Bread Man*. London: Universal Edition.

Holdstock, J. (1981c) *The Musicians of Bremen*. London: Universal Edition.

Holdstock, J. and Pitts, J. (1983) *Class Music from the Beginning*. Leeds: E.J. Arnold.

Hunt, B. (ed.) (1984) *Count Me In: 44 Songs and Rhymes about Numbers*. London: A. & C. Black.

Lewin, O. (1974) *Brown Girl in de Ring*. Oxford: Oxford University Press.

Lewin, O. (1975) *Beeny Bud*. Oxford: Oxford University Press.

McMorland, A. (ed.) (1978) *The Funny Family: Songs, Rhymes and Games for Children*. London: Ward Lock Educational.

Matterson, E. (1969) *This Little Puffin: Finger Plays and Nursery Games*. Harmondsworth: Penguin.

Nordoff, P. and Robbins, C. (1962 and subsequently) *Children's Playsongs*. Bryn Mawr, Pennsylvania: Presser.

Nordoff, P. and Robbins, C. (1968) *Fun for Four Drums*. Bryn Mawr, Pennsylvania: Presser.

Nordoff, P. and Robbins, C. (1972) *Spirituals*. Bryn Mawr, Pennsylvania: Presser.
Piper, B. I. (1982) *Sing as You Grow*. London: Ward Lock Educational.
Turnbull, J. (1980) *Just Me: A Song Book for Children*. Oxford: Oxford University Press.
Vajda, C. (1974) *The Kodaly Way to Music*. London: Boosey and Hawkes.
Williamson, M. (1970) *The Snow Wolf*. London: Weinberger.

Books on music

Alvin, J. (1976) *Music for the Handicapped Child*. Oxford: Oxford University Press.
Alvin, J. (1978) *Music Therapy for the Autistic Child*. Oxford: Oxford University Press.
Alvin, J. (new ed. 1983) *Music Therapy*. London: John Clare Books.
Bailey, P. (1973) *They Can Make Music*. Oxford: Oxford University Press.
Clark, C. and Chadwick, D. (1980) *Clinically Adapted Instruments for the Multiply Handicapped*. St Louis: Magnus Music Baton.
Critchley, M. and Henson, R. A. (eds) (1977) *Music and the Brain: Studies in the Neurology of Music*. London: Heinemann Medical.
DES (1985) *Music from 5 to 16*. London: HMSO.
Dobbs, J. (ed.) *Music for Slow Learners*. London: Bedford Square Press.
Ginglend, D. R. and Stiles, W. (1981) *Music Activities for Retarded Children*. Nashville: Abingdon Press.
Nordoff, P. and Robbins, C. (1971) *Therapy in Music for Handicapped Children*. London: Gollancz.
Nordoff, P. and Robbins, C. (1975) *Music Therapy in Special Education*. Plymouth: Macdonald and Evans.
Nordoff, P. and Robbins, C. (1978) *Creative Music Therapy*. New York: Day/London: Harper and Row.
Ward, D. (1976) *Hearts and Hands and Voices: Music in the Education of the Slow Learner*. Oxford: Oxford University Press.
Ward, D. (1979) *Sing a Rainbow: Musical Activities with Mentally Handicapped Children*. Oxford: Oxford University Press.
Wisbey, A. (1982) *Learn to Sing to Learn to Read*. London: BBC.

Further information

Music News is issued by the Disabled Living Foundation, 380 Harrow Road, London W9.

Music in Action is issued by the UK Council for Music Education and Training in association with Able Children (Pullen Publications) Ltd.

Silver Burdett Music Scheme is available in the UK through Mary Maggs, 25 Lipscombe Close, Newbury, Berkshire, RG14 5JW.

Music Therapy and Musical Speech Therapy Programme is available from Claus Bang, Aalborgskolen, Kollegievej 1, PO Box 7930, DK-9210 Aalborg, SØ, Denmark.

—5——————————————————

Art and Craft

Keith Chantry

RATIONALE

'What makes these kids so special and what can I do about it?' The first point we need to stress is that children with special educational needs are normal. This may seem rather an obvious point but in fact the many misconceptions and folkloric half-truths that colour our perceptions of these children often prevent our well intentioned efforts from bearing fruit. Strange as it may seem much of the folklore seems to cluster in the area of art and craft. Many of us, feeling somewhat beleaguered by recent developments in the education of children with special needs, tend to cling to simplistic analyses of need that hinder rather than help.

Recent research undertaken by Croll and Moses (1985) highlights many of the misconceptions we entertain concerning the nature of learning difficulty. It would seem that, in general, we tend to identify all children experiencing difficulty in reading as slow learners and that we are inclined to expect poor performance from them in other areas of the curriculum. This perception is further consolidated by our resolute disdain for diagnostic assessment procedures and our preference for our own subjective responses. The implications of the research seem to be that, in spite of our best intentions, and possibly because of large class sizes and lack of time, we are apt, quite wrongly, to stereotype children with learning difficulties and are likely to conjure up all sorts of false expectations that build in failure.

The problem with stereotyping is that it is beguiling and persuasive in its simplicity, but ultimately it bears little truth and is, at best, unhelpful. Consider such national stereotypes as 'all Englishmen wear bowler hats and carry rolled umbrellas'. Some of my American friends were seriously disconcerted to find this was not the case. We may find this faintly ridiculous and yet continue to entertain similar expectations of children with special needs. We imagine that they form ideally homogeneous groups requiring identical treatments. Let us examine some of these misconceptions and then look at some case studies that may serve to highlight the disparity that exists between truth and fiction.

Popular fictions

Children with special needs have no creativity or imagination

It is often assumed that children who cannot fluently express themselves in terms of images have no feelings or ideas to express. How often have we seen children with special needs in a primary classroom engaged in the most mundane and repetitive of tasks during an art session? We find them filling in areas of colour; sticking crushed tissue paper into predesignated areas. It is true that they are fully occupied; that they cannot make much of a mess. Their lack of co-ordination cannot spoil a piece of important display work. However they are not engaged in the tremendous exploration of self and environment that constitutes the phenomenon we call art. By saddling these children with the most banal of tasks we deny them the full flowering of sensibility that is the right of all our children. It is true that some children with learning difficulties often have poor fine-motor control and lack the ability to organise themselves and their materials. They often appear to lack the ability to memorise procedures necessary for the appropriate mix of colours or choice of medium. However, it must be remembered that each of our children has his or her own unique perceptions and sensations even if he or she lacks the physical or cognitive apparatus necessary for their expression. We need to be sensitive to these children as individual personalities who, given the appropriate medium, can express their thoughts and feelings and so impinge upon their environment; can, indeed, move us by their visions of it if only we dare to value such visions.

Art for children with special needs is a form of occupational therapy

This view, despite arising out of well-intentioned sympathy, is potentially damaging and untruthful when applied as a general rule. We often tend to make the mistake of over-praising the results of any artistic endeavours engaged in by children with special needs. It is often assumed that all children with special needs derive a particular kind of benefit from merely engaging in the act of applying paint to paper. The results of their work are often viewed uncritically or sentimentally: the act itself is regarded as being cathartic and therapeutic. It must be remembered that few children achieve fluent expression without guidance. Our presence as facilitator is never more necessary than when helping a child to find his or her own expressive voice.

We must conclude that neither of the foregoing perceptions of children's needs in relation to art and craft is truly helpful. In the first instance it is assumed that children with learning difficulties are incapable of creative expression and are to be relegated to mundane and repetitive tasks. In the second instance children with learning difficulties are offered no critical guidance: merely a form of uncritical sentimentality. It is not suggested that these forms of stereotyping are entirely typical of primary classroom practice; merely that such stereotypes do exist and that to a greater or lesser degree they occasionally inform our teaching and blight the creative growth of some pupils. In both cases it is often assumed that skills teaching is likely to be unproductive and that results will probably not be comparable to those of mainstream children.

The issues raised by the foregoing discussion will be further highlighted and clarified by the following case studies.

Case studies

Kevin. Kevin could not read. He was awkward, timid and withdrawn. He appeared to need a disproportionate amount of direct physical emotional comfort from his teacher, if he was denied this he would often throw tantrums. He became, as you might imagine, a difficult child to manage in class. He continued to fail in school and to be a problem in class. Eventually, upon transfer, he found himself referred to a special needs unit attached to a secondary school. When he left that school he had obtained a very respectable grade in 'O'-level art. I showed some of his examination pieces to a group of teachers engaged in an in-service training course in special needs. They were astounded at the sensitivity of his expression. Many of his pieces concerned themselves with objects drawn from observation. He evinced a delicacy of perception and confidence of expression that was quite breathtaking. We were moved to ask ourselves why this sensibility, with its highly developed analytical perception and delicacy of expression, could flourish within the constraints of the 'O'-level examination and yet had failed to do so in the comparably freer atmosphere of the primary classroom.

We decided that had Kevin not been condemned to failure by his lack of reading ability then there was every possibility his creative potential would have been realised. When placed in an accepting atmosphere Kevin could flower as a unique personality who could express his own highly sophisticated perception of the universe. In fact his proficiency in his chosen medium was well in advance of that of any of his teachers.

Stephen. Stephen, at present, resides in a school for maladjusted children. Whilst in his primary school he was noted for his emotionally turbulent personality and for his failure to cope with the everyday demands of classwork. However, he developed a poetic sensibility, the expression of which very powerfully objectified the warring elements of his personality. The prognosis for his future development is good and this is in major part due to the way in which Stephen's teachers have nurtured this capacity.

Stephen welded together the written word, images that were powerful, beautiful and, for him, in some sense formed an explanation of his responses to his environmnent. In this way he objectified his situation and created out of it something whole, unique and life affirming.

One of the characters in Stephen's fiction was *the moon-beam boy* who was visited by angels on occasion and was able to travel through time and space. His other character was *Nasty Jim* who was distinguished by his unpleasantness to his fellows but only managed to hurt himself. Stephen conjoined image and work with almost Blakeian facility and power and managed to comment with stunning maturity upon his own responses to his environment.

Mark. Mark is an extraordinarily practical boy. He helps the school caretaker to sweep leaves and generally to tidy the school. The caretaker regards him as a potential expert in this field. His academic work is extremely poor. At the age of 11 he is a virtual non-reader; his written work is largely illegible and his spelling ability non-existent. He seems unable to hold words in his memory for more than a few minutes for the purposes of either reading or writing. His motor co-ordination, both gross and fine, is very poor.

In art projects there was a tendency for him to be saddled with the most mundane and rudimentary of tasks; he would not be trusted to do more than draw around templates and fill in areas of colour.

However, despite his apparent shortcomings and poor level of skill acquisition, Mark's teacher has discovered that he could express his perception of his environment in a powerful, almost muscular fashion. Mark's class were engaged in drawing a bicycle from observation. Despite his motor-control problems, Mark was able to produce a complex, detailed drawing of the object that showed evidence of an understanding far beyond that which would normally have been expected from him. Despite the fact that lines were shaky and colour refused to stay within linear parameters his drawing displayed a grasp of the fundamental mechanics of bicycle engineering. His images had a powerful realism that illustrated an acute understanding of the relationship of the elements of the chosen object.

This drawing came as something of a revelation. Subsequent projects involving drawing from observation consolidated his teacher's new found respect for his vision. As a consequence of this appreciation Mark's imaginative work assumed greater confidence, coherence and muscle. Now he had found his voice, he was able to extend his repertoire to other sorts of image. Previously he had only ever drawn tractors (he came from a farming family). Attempts at other sorts of image had until then seemed to lack confidence and commitment. After seeing Mark's drawing of the bicycle his teacher's perception of his abilities has shifted dramatically and Mark's perceptions of his own abilities have altered similarly. Teacher and pupil now participate in once unexpected experiences of understanding.

Conclusion

None of these cases is in any way unique. Each child could have been condemned, because of a failure to cope with the fundamentals of primary classroom work in the area of language and reading, to mundane and repetitive work in art and craft lessons.

In each case a series of crucial experiences, facilitated by the understanding of a sensitive teacher, enabled these children to find their own creative voice. In each case these fresh understandings created opportunities for new learning and for the enhancement of mutual respect. Each individual was able to grow in stature: to assume new confidence and poise; to review his experience of the world afresh. In each case the sensitivity of the individual teacher was crucial in transforming the 'child with special needs' into an individual with unique insight. As you may imagine, these children tended to perform better in other curricular areas as a result of their experiences in the area of art and craft.

It could be argued, though, that these children are exceptional, special, not truly representative. You may wish to suggest that in the main children with special learning needs are lacking in imagination and execution. I would like to suggest, however, that these instances merely serve to highlight the fact that in general we underestimate the abilities of children with special needs; that we assume a pervasive lack of ability on the basis of shortfall in one curricular area. There is a similar temptation to make false assumptions concerning the creative potential of children with physical and sensory disabilities. There is a tendency to underestimate abilities on the basis of poor performance, and to allow the presence of handicap to persuade one that such children have no emotional and intellectual insights to express. It is merely that we have not yet provided the *modus operandi* whereby such expression can take place.

Likewise it is a common habit to overprotect such children, denying them the sort of stimulating experiences that could allow expression to develop. Yet there is really little problem in maximising their creative potential provided that the teacher ensures that clarity of communication is established (particularly for the hearing impaired) and that experiences are appropriately matched to the child's needs: a strong tactile element is important for the visually handicapped; activities must be within the manual motor range of the physically handicapped.

We cannot offer the foolproof trouble-shooting guide more commonly found in car maintenance manuals. The cases quoted earlier serve to remind us that the truly sensitive teacher can initiate the flowering of an individual child's sensibility and thus enhance his self concept. We are not advocating that any child should be allowed either time or privilege beyond the ordinary classroom curriculum limits. We would merely suggest that each child was entirely unexceptional but that an alteration in the perception of all the teachers involved was responsible for providing the children with experiences of challenge. The sensitive teacher can, within the context of the normal primary classroom, organise experiences that will provide sufficient challenge to lead children towards their own personal adventure. The teacher, sensitised to the need of his or her children, is able to perceive promise in the images resulting from experiences, to appraise them and to begin to enhance the potential perceived.

Recent developments in the teaching of children with special needs have attempted to provide just the sort of guides and sequential instructional procedures that would appear to obviate either pupil or teacher failure. It is suggested that, with a precise, sequential approach to teaching accompanied by task analysis, all our problems of teacher and pupil frustration will be resolved. In a later section we will suggest that, though these techniques are useful in the teaching of certain skills in the area of art and craft, the greater goal that we seek is unobtainable by these methods. I had occasion to visit a special school entirely devoted to such an approach to the curriculum. The teacher in charge of the art department resolutely resisted any attempts to implement the measures within her own department. The work produced in that department was so outstanding that none dared to venture that a change of approach was either practicable or desirable.

Margaret Donaldson in her very sensible and intelligent volume *Children's Minds* suggests that a prescriptive, skills-based approach to the curriculum assumes that in order to begin to learn effectively children with special needs must never experience failure. She points out that if this be the case these children will never experience challenge or adventure. In the cases we have delineated the children set the parameters of their own endeavour; on no occasion were they set tasks wherein there was an objective criterion of failure or success. They were able, therefore, to engage in their own learning experience, free to determine their own criteria of success. The crucial factor, as we have seen, was the sensitivity of the teacher responsible for them. No packaged learning aid or prescriptive teaching manual could build in the sort of flexibility that would allow these sort of phenomena to occur.

CURRICULUM MATTERS

'Okay I'm sensitive and caring, but what do I do now?' We have now made our way through the minefield of myths that tend to cluster around any discussion of art and special needs. We have also outlined how the experience of art has a necessary place in the education of children with special needs. We have tried to show that this experience is crucial to the development of sensitive, mature young people and have tentatively suggested that even children with special needs may find that skills developed in this curricular area may be as useful in earning a living in future life as skills developed in other areas.

It so often happens that art is viewed by teachers as some form of non-serious, low-status activity that occurs on a Friday afternoon when language and number routines have been successfully completed. Each session appears to bear little relationship to previous painting sessions. There would appear to be no discernible thematic link with other curricular experiences. Too often, emphasis is placed upon the acquisition of basic skills in the area of language and reading, particularly with children with learning difficulties. It is, of course, important that these skills should be acquired, but not if it leads to the impoverishment we so frequently witness in other areas of the curriculum. It could be suggested that a severely unbalanced curricular diet endangers the future mental health of children. This may sound a little far-fetched to some readers, but my own experiences of the behaviour of children exposed to a narrow and restricted curriculum in which creative potential is stifled suggest that they tend to react negatively towards the institution responsible for their curricular diet.

Discussions concerning the curriculum often appear to lack immediacy or excitement. Teachers and students find it difficult not to yawn when faced with pages of white A4 paper decorated with curriculum models and diagrams. We feel reality slipping away from us and we are tempted to ask 'What can all this have to do with teaching and learning as we know it? How can these matrices and pie charts enable us to function more effectively at 9.30 on Monday morning?' It is a somewhat sad truism that children with special educational needs are more dependent upon our organisation and development of the curriculum than their more able peers. This is not to suggest, conversely, that bright children need little teaching and can almost teach themselves although this may have become almost an accepted item of teacher folklore. It is possible, however, to make a general statement to the effect that in many cases children with special needs seem not to be very good at learning incidentally. They seem not to be able to make connections between learned items as effectively as other children. Often they seem only able to learn that which we deliberately set out to teach them directly. They are, it seems, in this respect far more vulnerable, far more at our mercy in that they are more dependent upon us for their learning experiences. We have a greater obligation, therefore, to engage in rigorous systematic planning in order to ensure that our art curriculum can be seen to be coherent and developmental. At the same time we need to be sensitive enough to the responses children make to the experiences we present to enlarge upon a topic that engages their attention and we need to be professional enough to abandon one that does not.

What is, in essence, being suggested is that we continue planning and organisation with flexibility and sensitivity, that we ensure that creative and aesthetic experiences are available for all in our curriculum, and that we take the time and trouble to organise our art curriculum with an eye to the development of themes over a period of time. It is important that we treat art with the same sort of seriousness that we afford to mathematics and language; that we spend time developing a course of study or a series of experiences for all of our children and that we can justify our engagement in those experiences. Such a course of study should ideally balance thematic development, personal expression and skill acquisition. There should exist sufficient coherence between sessions for the child to establish links with past experiences and to plan for future ones. The child should be able to build a repertoire of skills and to acquire a visual vocabulary culled from significant artistic experiences.

All that seems to be asked for is that all of our children leave school as better artists than they were when they first arrived. We take time to ensure that this is the case in other areas of the curriculum; we worry if a child fails to read or to make the sort of progress we feel he should be making. We worry if her spelling or handwriting do not improve. If a child fails to grasp decomposition of tens and units, we work very hard to ensure that he eventually does so or we call in outside agencies. We too often fail to see the need to teach art in an organised and individualised basis, never worrying if artistic concepts fail to be grasped, if skills are not acquired.

In some areas of the curriculum, salvation appears to be offered by behaviourist curriculum developers. They offer seemingly foolproof systematic routines that prevent children with special needs ever having to experience failure. One can readily purchase survival kits that purport to diagnose and remediate in such a structured fashion that all our classroom organisational problems relating to special needs would appear to be at an end. Thankfully art is one curricular area that seems to have escaped the attentions of this group – and for very good reasons. Beguiling though the workshop manuals may appear to be, they have failed to consider a dynamic central to continued effective learning, particularly in the area of art: that is, risk taking. Fortunately, so much artistic experience involves risk taking and challenge that the art curriculum remains free of some of the more rigidly prescriptive initiatives in other curricular areas.

Building the curriculum

From our examination of the experience of individual children and our discussion of children's experience of the curriculum, it is possible to extract certain basic principles that should guide our planning of an art curriculum for children with special needs.
1. Children with special needs have as much right as their peers to partake in the adventure of artistic experience.
2. The learning that takes place in art is as valuable as that which takes place in other areas of the curriculum.
3. This being the case, the art curriculum deserves as much careful planning and development for individual needs as other areas.
4. Children with special needs can perform as well as their peers in this curricular dimension but are far more dependent upon the teacher as facilitator to organise a coherent course of study.
Once it is established that we are sensitive to the aptitudes and perceptions of children with special needs and that we are agreed that artistic experience is crucial to the development of all children, we must proceed to consider exactly what we shall teach and how we can make that material accessible to all the children in our care.

Surviving at the chalkface: disaster avoidance strategies
(Welcome to the real world)

So far we have suggested that children with special needs do not form a homogeneous group who differ markedly from other children. We have noted that, given certain conditions, children with special needs have similar sensitivities and perceptions to those possessed by all children. Furthermore, it should not be inferred that because a child fails to read, he or she is necessarily a slow learner in every area of the curriculum. In the past we have tended to label and stereotype children in the primary school on the basis of performance in one or more curricular areas. This is likely to be a damaging and unfruitful activity. It should be possible for the ordinary classroom teacher to capitalise upon the creative potential of all children and to facilitate artistic development. There are likely to be problems, but certain practical measures, if undertaken, help to prevent such problems from disrupting a carefully planned lesson. We need to generate a model that can be applied to all areas of the art curriculum. The questions we need to ask before we begin any activity are:

1. Why am I doing this?
2. What am I trying to teach?
3. How does it relate to what went before and what will come after?
4. What skills am I assuming?

If we were to apply this scrutiny to all of our activities, it is unlikely that we should experience the sort of frustrations that so often occur when we have spent hours preparing a lesson only to find that many children use inappropriate materials, make a thorough mess and finish the task in no seconds flat.

It does pay dividends to engage in a process of task analysis before embarking upon a particular project. It may be that you have presupposed that your children have engaged in certain experiences that in reality they have not. Certain key elements that we shall touch upon in the following sections include the appropriate use of media, the acquisition of techniques and the adequate use of language by teachers to direct children and to describe tasks. We shall also examine the use of language as an instrument that can enable children to integrate past experiences with present ones. Too often, it would seem, art is a solitary activity that would benefit from group discussion; the sharing of responses to problem-solving situations. We shall address these questions whilst considering a variety of dimensions of the art curriculum.

The drawing lesson

If we take as our example an apparently straightforward lesson whereby we ask our children to create an image on paper based upon their observations of an object or collection of objects we can obtain some idea of the sort of problems and issues that may be built in to such a situation and by extension to all the activities we ask children to undertake.

Before we begin:
* Do the children understand which materials you wish them to use?
* Can you rely upon each child to have a sensitivity to the materials appropriate for the task?
* Does each child know the difference between a hard and soft pencil?
* Is each child aware of the repertoire of marks, images and effects that it is possible to create with the chosen materials?
* Are you going to allow freedom of choice of material and strategy or should you direct and guide?

Traditionally we have tended to devise drawing from observation situations and collect the result without stopping to consider the sort of issues outlined above. We have somehow felt that by doing so we were allowing children maximum freedom of expression. Anything else, we were wont to think, is likely to constitute interference resulting in a stifling of creativity. My own feeling is that children, particularly those with special needs, are unlikely to grow in terms of creative expression unless we prepare, direct, intervene and demonstrate when appropriate. In some situations I feel we can apply the sort of strategies that we would utilise in the areas of maths or science. We are engaged in a problem-solving situation; we should be happy therefore to demonstrate strategies that may lead to the resolution of a problem. We can endeavour, both as a group and individually, to talk through the experience, comparing individual responses to visual problems and discussing how we might successfully interpret three-dimensional reality upon a two-dimensional surface.

As has been suggested, we should not feel afraid to guide and to present possible solutions to the problem of visual representation. We are, I hasten to add, not determining the final result but merely ensuring that some learning takes place, ensuring that the children are able to look and select from their environment and then to interpret that experience in terms of marks upon paper.

Described thus, we can appreciate the complexity of the operation in which we are inviting children to engage. Children with special needs are likely to need guidance in such situations. It is possible that they would choose inappropriate materials and produce hurried and rudimentary images if left entirely to their own devices. They may misunderstand the requirements of the task.

All children are likely to be capable of improving their drawing skill and of developing a range of skills and techniques in order to express their developing vision. However, as with many other activities engaged in by children at school, it is necessary that both teacher and child appreciate the demands made by a particular situation. The teacher needs to be aware of the skills and expertise required to complete a chosen task successfully and needs to seek actively to develop them. In this particular situation we are hoping to develop the critical observation of objects in the environment and to aid the children in expressing a critical perception of those objects. Following this it is vitally important that we capitalise upon such experiences by exposing the children to more challenging and complex situations. The medium of language will help us to make that move. Through group discussion we can relate previous experiences to new ones comparing strategies and techniques. We can then proceed to experiment with different media for representing objects on paper: ink and wash or charcoal and chalk.

We can begin to see that from a single session of drawing from observation we can develop a course of study that allows all children to build upon experiences, to develop a variety of skills and to refine their critical perceptions. By group discussion and comparison of results we enable each other to share the experience of visual problem solving. One can guarantee that no two images will be alike, each child being engaged in developing a personal vision and mode of expression.

There is no reason, given the forethought and support that has been suggested, why children with special needs should not be able to share equally in the sort of experiences described. The following suggestions should be of some help in enabling all of the children to derive maximum benefit from a drawing session.

1. Carefully consider the language in which your instructions are couched. Are you assuming concepts and terminology unfamiliar to some of the children?

2. Analyse the skills necessary for the successful completion of the task. Can each child hold a pencil correctly? Should you allow free choice of materials? Does each child know what to look at or how to look? It has not been unknown for children engaged in this sort of task to be seen copying from one another rather than from the object. Obviously for some, the notion of rendering three-dimensional form in two dimensions can be a wholly new and intimidating situation. When there is a misunderstanding of the nature of the task there is security in copying from one's neighbour.

3. Do not at first be over concerned with the resulting images. In this case it is the process of looking we are trying to foster and the learning that may accrue from it. With a subject such as mathematics we are often at pains to emphasise the fact that we are not over concerned with pupils achieving correct answers. It is the *process* of problem solution that indicates *quality* of thinking and conceptual development. If we

emphasise this aspect of our endeavours, we should not experience the sort of destructive behaviour that results from a recognition of one's own inadequacy.

4. Above all, value the responses each individual makes to the situation. As we have suggested, there are no 'right' answers and our criterion of success at first should not be how well the resulting images may decorate our display board. We have promoted the idea of group discussion and comparison of individual responses. This should be undertaken not in a spirit of competition or striving for a 'right' answer. Rather it should be an opportunity for all to share their response to a situation.

5. Do ensure that you build upon these experiences. If this learning experience is only a 'one-off', it is likely that any learning will be lost. It is up to us to enable children to integrate past experiences with present and future ones. This allows them to grow in skill and to assemble a repertoire of devices useful for solving problems of visual perception. Such a repertoire will enable them to engage more fruitfully in imaginative representation.

The painting lesson

If we intend to use paint it is important that we ensure that all children know:

1. When to use a large brush and when to use a small one.
2. When to use paint thickly or thinned with water.
3. How much paint to load upon the brush.

It is unreasonable to expect a child to know how to create a colour wash unless he or she has been taught how to do so. Similarly, fine detailed work cannot be accomplished using a large bristled brush.

It is not sensible to expect children to mix colours readily unless they have been taught how to do so. Many inexperienced children cannot predict what the result of mixing particular colours is likely to be. It is worth while, for a period of time, to restrict the range of colours available, thereby ensuring that the children will need to ask you how to 'make' green or pink or purple. They will only be able to predict possible outcomes when colours are used in combination if they have experienced this before. Far more powerful learning will take place if the children themselves discover the need to create new colours rather than being instructed to do so as part of a formal paint mixing session. It is highly likely that children with learning difficulties could success-fully mix paints in such a formal session, but when engaged in painting a picture will revert to using colours straight from the pot.

Very often we expect children to know how to do certain things when it is likely that they have never been taught how and, as has been suggested, many children with special needs do not learn unless we deliberately, directly teach them. We also need to help them to transfer techniques learned in one session to other situations. We tend at times, moreover, to underestimate the complexity of the problems posed by visual representation. As we have seen, colour mixing requires the child to choose colours, to keep his brush clean when mixing them, to note the outcome, to store that information in his memory and to be able to retrieve it at some later time when it is required.

My own experience leads me to believe that memory retrieval is one facet of human behaviour that often differentiates the able from the slow learner. As teachers we have to provide sufficient support to prevent that expression being impeded. If there is one single message that underpins this chapter it is likely to be this: creative expression should be fluent and successful, allowing the child to create something with its own identity and beauty. Children with special needs are able to do this if we recognise their potential difficulties and circumvent them whilst still leaving the child with some element of challenge to face.

We need to recognise that some children are often thwarted by the organisational requirements of a painting session and in the light of this we might list some potential disaster areas.

1. Choosing colours: has the child picked too many or too few? Has he or she become so involved in sorting out this problem as to be unlikely ever to get started?
2. Table organisation: is the water jar where he or she can knock it over thereby creating disruption? Will he or she know when to change the water?
3. Brush etiquette: does the child realise that you need to clean your brush between colours? Has he or she chosen appropriate sized brushes for the job? Will he or she realise when to use a colour wash and when to use paint thickly? Will he or she over or under load the brush?
4. The horror of the white page: some children are intimidated by a large white sheet of paper and will spend most of the session time fiddling in a corner of the paper. It is often useful to use off-white paper that has been previously covered with a light wash.
5. Procedure: children frequently do not know where to start on a painting. They will fill in details only to find that the larger areas of colour will obliterate these. They start on the most interesting areas without realising that in doing so they create untold burdens for themselves.

The light craft session

It is here, probably more than anywhere else, that teachers of children with special needs find that they are in danger of losing their sanity. Not only do we have to battle with conceptual problems but with the perceptual and motor co-ordination problems that children with special needs seem to possess in unfair proportion. We need to be particularly careful that the language we use to direct children and to instruct them is in accord with their perceptions and understanding. Classroom organisation is likely to be of paramount importance. Children with special needs are unlikely to be able to complete tasks within groups aided only by verbal instruction. You are likely to be required to work very closely with these children and to demonstrate any techniques you wish to see applied. This may affect your lesson preparation and classroom organisation to a not inconsiderable degree. While involved in such tasks one becomes aware of the inadequacy of language to convey certain types of information accurately. Quite often the teacher will be required to demonstrate actively to each child individually how to accomplish a task. Considerations of this nature may have implications for the organisation of such sessions.

It will probably be useful here, as in previous sections, to create a list of possible pitfalls in order that one may plan for success.
1. Paper/card folding: often difficult for the child with poor co-ordination. It can be quite a difficult task for some children to fold a piece of paper in half so that both halves are equal. As we have suggested, it may be that mere verbal descriptions are inadequate. You may need to allow the child to experiment with several 'practice' pieces before the task can be success-fully accomplished.
2. Using a ruler: it is not unusual to find that children cannot measure and cannot appreciate that a mark made at a measured point needs to be precisely located. Drawing a line between two points can often prove difficult. You may find that you need to teach how to hold a ruler so that it does not move when a line is drawn along it.
3. Using a craft knife: remember that children can have difficulty in sorting out which is the cutting edge and will resolve the difficulty the hard way unless prevented, leading to a shedding of blood and maximum class disruption.
4. Scissor work: it is useful to try and ensure that you have decent pointed scissors that are neither stiff nor blunt. There is nothing so frustrating as having poor tools for any job.
In these sorts of sessions it is useful if you can work with a small group of children and if you can work closely with them. Otherwise

you will need to analyse the task carefully beforehand to try and anticipate the sort of pitfalls outlined and prevent them from threatening the smooth running of your lesson.

Forward planning

It is likely that at some point you will feel the need to organise your thinking and to prepare a course of study for the month, term or year ahead. At this stage planning is likely to be devoted to general areas of study rather than the details of individual sessions.

Ultimately we need to be striving to achieve a balance between the various elements of our art curriculum. Skill acquisition and self expression constantly compete for our attention. How much time do we devote to the nuts and bolts of image making? Do we concentrate on formal technique or do we allow children to try and solve formal problems as they occur? In this instance it is essential that the balance be maintained. The acquisition of skills must ever be subservient to the expression of thoughts, ideas and feelings. It is true that without a diversity of skills the fluent expression of ideas is hampered. However, if we teach an entirely skills-based curriculum we are likely to arrive at a situation where we have a number of children who can perform a certain number of 'tricks' to order. Whether or not they have the wherewithal to apply them appropriately in a non-directed situation is another matter. Anyone can be taught techniques that, rather joylessly employed, result in a not unpleasant image. This should not be confused with artistic creation. It may be, however, that a child is unable to realise his or her internal conceptions due to lack of skill or technique. Without guidance, direction and perception on the part of the teacher it is unlikely that realisation will occur.

Experimentation with materials can obviously be great fun, but we should not be deceived into thinking that these experiences alone can lead a child towards the fluent expression of artistic statements. If we merely teach skills or provide opportunities for media experiments we are hoping that children will somehow make imaginative connections between these experiences and deploy them effectively at some future time. Unfortunately children with learning difficulties are unlikely to make those connections. They often fail to learn incidentally and any activity that in some way leads us away from the creative act of expressing thoughts and feelings is unhelpful. It may be that such sessions are fun and indeed may be seen to be therapeutic in some way, in that case they should be valued for what they are and not confused with the real practice of art. In conclusion, we should beware of confusing games and tricks with the real business of art. Children with special needs, without our guidance, may never develop the discrimination to marry technique and media to their conceptions.

In our planning it is important that we achieve a balance between media exploration, skill acquisition and expression. The major emphasis should always be upon guiding our children towards fluent creative expression. Skills and media are means by which we create powerful images. We are hopeful that our children can appreciate and discriminate between effective and poor designs – that they develop an aesthetic sense that will allow them to create statements that express thought and feeling and display an appreciation of composition and design. These things cannot, of course, be taught in the same way as brush or pencil skills, but when planning, it is useful to remember that they are our ultimate aims.

When the inherent balance of a proposed programme has been decided upon, it becomes necessary further to decide upon the content of the art sessions. It is often useful to try to aim for some sort of thematic link between art sessions. A strongly determined theme or topic can provide the dynamic necessary to integrate skill teaching with expressive work. A strongly developed theme or topic can determine skills to be taught and media to be experimented with and can be further developed by the responses of the children.

Projects

The operation of a thematic programme can best be illustrated by a first-hand description of a project. The adoption of a project approach could integrate those elements of the art curriculum we have explored previously. The project structure allows sufficient flexibility for the needs of all children to be catered for. What follows is the documentary record of a project undertaken by myself and a group of primary age children. The aim is to illustrate how a project could be structured in order to help those engaged in the planning and preparation of courses.

My primary aim was to introduce the children to the processes and operations usually undertaken by artists contemplating the creation of a large piece of work. The group I had chosen to work with would not, I surmised, be used to the idea of developing an image over a period of time. I decided that we could examine a tract of land adjacent to the school and try to depict it utilising a variety of techniques. The culmination of the project would be the bringing together of previous experiences when the final piece was attempted.

The first thing I had considered when devising the project was the content of the group's art curriculum prior to embarking upon this particular course of study. It appeared that in the main they had experienced art sessions as individual and distinct events. It was not expected that they should make connections between these disparate events. It was unlikely that there would be any accumulation of skills accruing from such experiences as no such expectation underpinned the planning of their course of study.

My second consideration was the distribution of ability throughout the group. In order to assess this information I consulted with teachers who had been involved with this particular group of children. I was able to ascertain that the group consisted of children from both rural and urban backgrounds and that there was a large number of children who had experienced some form of learning difficulty. Ideally, the project would be accessible to all, irrespective of ability level.

The first phase of the operation consisted of asking the children to make a pencil drawing of the piece of land in question. It consisted of hedgerows, a field and a foreground densely packed with grasses, thistles and wild flowers. Afterwards when we gathered together we placed all the images side by side and proceeded to look at how each of us had solved the problem of representing such a scene.

On the following day I instructed the children to revisit the field equipped with pastels and pencil crayons. On this occasion we were concerned to make a colour sketch of the scene. I encouraged the children to make verbal and visual notes on paper to record colour distribution across the composition, e.g. light green for the grass nearest to us, dark green for the hedgerow. Following this we again gathered together, placed the images side by side and discussed results.

The next session saw us mixing colours in an attempt to replicate those we had perceived in the previous sessions. Successful mixes were marked and we attempted to keep a record of how we had arrived at them. In the final session we worked on large images of the landscape we had been studying. Colour washes were found to be an effective method of depicting skies. Several pupils tried using pastels to create the subtle gradations and textures of a large expanse of grass. The immediate foreground, which comprised grasses, wild flowers and thistles, seemed to be best dealt with by utilising pencils and pen and ink.

All of the images that resulted from this project, sketches, washes, colour mixes and verbal notes, were displayed alongside the final landscape images to great effect.

A number of weeks later the group were instructed to take themselves around the school and choose some scene to depict visually. In some ways this was to be an informal assessment for me of how much learning had been taken on board by the children during the project. Surprisingly, they did not merely repeat the images of the previous sessions in a rehashed, clichéd manner, but created new images that incorporated some of the techniques learnt in previous episodes.

The primary aim of this project was not to create a beautiful display for visitors to admire (although ultimately our sessions provided us with just this), but to try to teach the children how to look at their environment. We also attempted to equip them with a variety of techniques that would enable them to realise their responses to their environment.

Throughout the project we would gather together to discuss our results. Group discussion became an inseparable part of our process of working. Art can be a very solitary occupation and each individual's work is often impoverished by such solitude. I endeavoured, and to some extent succeeded, to create the atmosphere of a workshop or studio. This in itself would be seen as an important dynamic in the artistic process.

This then was the pattern of our landscape project:

1. Preliminary sketches in pencil;
2. Group discussion of results;
3. Colour sketches in pastel and crayon;
4. Group discussion of results;
5. Colour-mixing experiments;
6. Group discussion of results;
7. Drawing from observation in pen and ink of individual grasses, flowers, etc.;
8. Group discussion of results;
9. Final mixed-media piece;
10. Display of all elements of project;
11. Non-directed individual landscape painting session.

This pattern lent itself well to a further project concerned with portraits and figure drawing. We worked upon a variety of subjects including self portraits, portraits of friends, portraits depicting a variety of emotions and also caricatures.

We can see that the model attempts to create a balance between those elements that could be deemed to be essential to the creation of art while recognising that skill acquisition and media experimentation must always be serving a purpose. Throughout the course of the project we attempted to provide a strong thematic link between each of the experiences in recognition of the fact that isolated experiences result in learning that quickly decays. It was also possible to tailor the project to individual needs; to allow children to pursue particular experiences more than once, to allow others to miss out phases and proceed to others. Gradually all members of the group made the project their own and found freedom enough to pursue their own obsessions and discover their own skill requirements.

While I was involved in running the project, I took the opportunity of engaging in some research. The intention of this investigation was to assess the visual learning capabilities of children with special needs in a somewhat rigorous fashion. Two groups of children, one with special needs, were asked to draw objects from observation and to apply the visual data accrued from these experiences at some later date. The results of the experiments demonstrated that, although operating at different levels of sophistication, both groups were able to abstract visual information from a situation and that the learning that accrued was durable enough to be applied at some considerable time later. It would appear, therefore, that it is reasonable to construct a thematic programme of study and to expect all children, irrespective of ability, to learn from it.

A curriculum model

We would thus far conclude that the following elements would, of necessity, form part of an art curriculum designed for primary-aged children. The question of facilitating access for children with special needs has been discussed in previous sections and the following recommendations are envisaged to be appropriate for children of all abilities.

Looking

Very young children tend to create images comprised of stereotypes: houses and people are depicted in a single fashion. These stereotypes seem to be common to children of all classes and races. By junior-age level the children are usually ready to interact with the world and to engage in problem-solving activities: creating images that reconcile three-dimensional reality with a two-dimensional surface. We can foster this ability by creating situations wherein such problem-solving strategies are called into play. Drawing from observation is one such situation. Individualised guidance plus group discussion enables children with special needs to derive maximum benefit from situations of this sort.

Media exploration

Too often children appear to explore the potential of different media in a shallow and transitory manner. We must remember that the medium should always meet an expressive need. If we teach on an individualised basis we should be able to assess the response of a child and guide him or her towards the appropriate medium. In short the medium should be a vehicle by which the child realises on paper his or her mental image. Our job is to try and assess that internal image and to facilitate its appearance upon paper.

Continuity and coherence

If one operates a project-based curriculum continuity and coherence are obviously easier to achieve than if one does not. However, even if another method is adopted, if one plans carefully and continues to evaluate children's responses to situations then it should not be difficult to build upon previously acquired skills. What should be remembered is that children with special needs may find it difficult to make connections between disparate events. We need to ensure that there is an observable continuity and coherence built into our art curriculum. Much of our experience tells us that children with special needs respond well to teaching. They cannot be relied upon, however, always to make connections and discover their own learning unless well supported in the act.

CONCLUSIONS

Essentially, what is being suggested is that all children, regardless of their ability, should be allowed to engage in the business of art in much the same way as an artist would. We need to be serious about art not unlike the way we are serious about English and Mathematics. We recognise that in these latter areas we need to assess and develop individual strengths. We often fail to treat the art curriculum with comparable seriousness and thereby fail our pupils by giving art a low status. We should not just be serving the needs of the display area, nor should we be filling in time in some semblance of occupational therapy. At one extreme we are in danger of valuing presentation more highly than the development of the children, while at the other extreme we may not value the images the children produce but imagine that the process of manufacture in some way contributes to their wellbeing. That said, it must be noted that children appreciate their work being attractively displayed and that for some children the process of manufacture *is* therapeutic and important. As in many areas of the curriculum we should work towards a balance and avoid extremes.

We have attempted to show that children with special needs can engage in visual learning just as well as other children. They may, at first, appear to operate at a less sophisticated level, but given appropriate supportive teaching they may be allowed to realise their vision.

Nevertheless, we would do well to remember that we generalise at our peril. Children with special needs do not form a readily identifiable homogeneous group within any classroom. They do not exhibit entirely similar habits and identical styles of learning. Children with learning difficulties may have problems with the organisation of materials and the stringing together of previously taught skills, equally children with perceptual and motor problems need particular kinds of support. The partially-hearing child may need individual supportive instruction. The partially-sighted child may need to be guided towards activities that do not require a perceptual acuity she or he can never possess. The emotionally disturbed child may attempt to spoil either his or her work or the work of others and may be particularly prone to frustration. Your planning should take into account these possible responses for careful planning and sensitivity to children's responses are likely to be the factors that will enhance the performance of all children within the normal primary classroom, whatever their strengths or areas of difficulty.

REFERENCES

Croll, P. and Moses, D. (1985) *One in Five*. London: Routledge & Kegan Paul.
Donaldson, M. (1982) *Children's Minds*. London: Fontana.

FURTHER READING AND RESOURCES

BBC (1984) *Look, Look and Look Again*. London: BBC Publications. This programme provides a useful stimulus to any art course. The teachers' notes are an excellent source of project ideas.
Eisner, E. W. (1972) *The Mythology of Art Education*. Falmer: Brighton Polytechnic. This provides excellent food for thought. Eisner debunks any number of myths that have bedevilled art education for years.
Figg, G. (1985) In search of a primary art curriculum. *Journal of Art and Design* 4 (1). This article is full of practical suggestions for planning curriculum: some of the wisest thinking one may encounter when attempting to plan courses and projects.

Literature and special needs in the primary school

John Fitzpatrick

In the prologue to Hermann Hesse's novel *Demian* the narrator reflects: 'every man is not only himself, he is also the unique, particular, always significant and remarkable point where the phenomena of the world intersect once and for all and never again'. The extraordinary singularity of each individual being, which Hesse is here celebrating, is easily lost sight of. We are all prone to a glib labelling of others that is damaging in two main ways: it denies or limits the potential fullness of being of the person labelled, and it relieves the labeller of the necessary and demanding richness of response to that fullness. In using the term 'special needs' we must not make the mistake of designating a group of children as other, as being apart or different in their needs: in our uniqueness we are all special, we all have special needs. What it can alert us to is the fact that meeting some children's needs may require from us more patience, greater flexibility and deeper understanding.

There are, we are aware, children whose severity of disability calls for highly specialised teaching and equipment of a kind that is not being met currently in mainstream schools, and though much of what we have to say regarding literature and what it offers may well be applicable to those children, our main concern here is with the pupils in ordinary schools identified by both Warnock (1978) and teachers as being in need. Most particularly our concern is with those, the majority according to the survey carried out by Croll and Moses (1985), who are reluctant readers. Though a truism, it cannot be stressed too often that the centrality of reading in education means that failure to acquire the skill or lack of expertise in it becomes a major problem in itself and can seriously undermine the child's overall progress. Of course, children with special needs are not a single homogeneous group, and it is important to emphasise that in so far as literature, distinctively, speaks of and to our particularity, and of and to our common humanity, it has within it the means of providing for all of us an enriching source of shared experience, and is uniquely placed to meet every child's need.

But what do we mean by literature, and what are the needs that it meets? There is no simple definition of literature, and the word might seem overly portentous when applied to most of the imaginative works that children read in primary school. However, Daiches (1956) has a useful formula that indicates in general terms what we are referring to, though for our purposes it will have to be understood that wordless picture books are also included:

> Literature as we are here using the term refers to any kind of composition in verse or prose which has for its purpose not the communication of fact but the telling of a story (either wholly invented or given new life by invention) or the giving of pleasure through some use of the inventive imagination in the employment of words.

WHAT DOES LITERATURE OFFER?

For children who do take pleasure in literature what does it offer? Heeks (1981) has rightly pointed out that there is 'no blueprint we can turn to for analysis of children's needs and books appropriate to them'. Some years ago, when bibliotherapy was in the news, a cartoon appeared showing a tiny girl peering up at a librarian who is asking, 'And what is your problem?' The naive attitude that the cartoon mocks (every child a problem child, books as instant panaceas) is a salutary reminder of the danger of too simplistic an approach to the complex ways in which reader and book interrelate. If we think of needs in a deeper sense than immediate problems, though, and if we accept that the nature of the interaction between reader and text, and its effects, does not lend itself to incontrovertible and conclusive demonstration, we may still, by reflection on a range of readers' experiences, draw some valid inferences.

A useful starting point for our consideration suggests itself in the four major areas of children's needs that Kellmer Pringle (1974) has outlined:
1. the need for love and security;
2. the need for new experiences;
3. the need for praise and recognition;
4. the need for responsibility.

ANSWERING THE NEED FOR NEW EXPERIENCES

Of these four it is the second to which literature can most obviously make a special contribution. Any justification of literature in the curriculum will inevitably give high priority to the manifold ways in which it provides us with that plenitude and variety of experience, that feeling insight into other lives, other times, other cultures, that an ordinary life could never in reality encompass. In the novels of Laura Ingalls Wilder, for example, children can re-enter the pioneer world of the American West in the 1870s, sharing in both the warmth and stability of the family life depicted, and the numerous trials and hazards they encountered. Numerous landlocked city children have first savoured the pleasures of boating and the outdoor life in the novels of Arthur Ransome. The lasting popularity of *Black Beauty* reminds us of how powerfully books that create a sympathetic insight into the lives of other creatures can engage children's feelings. Alan Marshall's *I Can Jump Puddles* and Ivan Southall's *Let the Balloon Go* enable us to feel upon our pulses the lives of the disabled in ways both moving and richly educative. Fantasies such as *Flat Stanley* by Jeff Brown and *The Shrinking of Treehorn* by Florence Parry Heide speak in oblique but no less potent ways to children's fascination with their diminutive place in the world and the possibility of alternative lives. *Treehorn* also enacts with telling humour and invention the ways in which the adult world, while seeming to care, can remain blithely indifferent to the needs of children as they, the children, perceive them. Ted Hughes' hugely successful *The Iron Man* combines an absorbing narrative with an imaginative questioning of our attitudes to war and our stereotyped responses to things alien. Folk tales and poems such as *Tales for Reading Aloud* by Leila Berg and *I Din Do Nuttin and Other Poems* by John Agard, or the realistic short stories of Bernard Ashley's *I'm Trying to Tell You* offer the reader the positive images that are vital for a wider acceptance and greater understanding of the different cultures in our multiracial society.

ANSWERING THE NEED FOR LOVE AND SECURITY

Although sometimes viewed as mere escapism, a desire to find in books a compensation for the paucity of reality, an involvement with literature can be seen far more positively as a desire for wholeness. As Fischer (1963) states:

> Evidently man wants to be more than just himself. He is not satisfied with being a separate individual and out of the partiality of his individual life he strives towards a fullness of life of which individuality with all its limitations cheats him, towards a more comprehensible, a more just world, a world that makes sense.

In meeting our desire for wholeness and our urge to make sense of the world, literature would seem to be satisfying also the first of Kellmer Pringle's needs, the need for love and security, at least with regard to the child's wish for security. Of course, as parents and teachers well know, the sharing of stories with a child (or a group of children) can provide a loving and secure experience of a very special kind. In what ways, though, could it be said that stories in themselves meet the child's need for security? At the simplest level they make available to young children a representation of their world that they can enter safely, explore and savour, free of the oppressive sense of bewilderment they often feel when faced with the unpredictable contingency of the real world.

As Kellmer Pringle notes, because of the child's ignorance simple things such as water running out of a bath can be seen as frightening, and 'perhaps most of all the nature and strength of his own feelings threaten his security from time to time'. It is noteworthy in this connection that some of the picture/story books most popular with young children are those such as Maurice Sendak's *Where the Wild Things Are*, or David McKee's *Not Now, Bernard*, or Hiawyn Oram's *Angry Arthur*, where the child's anger with parents is depicted in forceful visual and symbolic forms.

Books offered to children in the early stages of their development will often mirror their day-to-day world, making it more accessible to them, providing them with what Robert Frost (1939) called in a memorable phrase 'a momentary stay against confusion', where there is time for reflection and a deepening of understanding. In experiencing at one remove what are likely to be familiar anxieties (fear of the dark, separation from a loved one, anger with parents) and pleasures (visits to relatives, the daily round, the delights of play) children are enabled to think about experience in ways that partake of the detachment and involvement that is a distinctive feature of our engagement with fictions. At the same time, in sensing their kinship with the lives of others they are presented with the means of escaping from the bonds of a narrow egocentricity. The delighted recognition of ourselves in others and others in ourselves is one of the most potent insights literature can afford; and though younger children are not likely to register such moments in quite the same conscious way that older children or adults might, the possibility is nevertheless there for an increased awareness of the shared lineaments of our disparate natures. White's (1954) journal of the books and picture books that she read to her daughter between the ages of 2 and 5 has numerous illustrations of the interpenetration of life and literature in the early experience of a young child. As Martin (1983) commenting on the journal says:

Stories provide a form through which children can hold their experiences together; not only the verbal forms which signal a story (once upon a time etc.) but characters, situations and events – those basic literary elements which are often archetypal images of patterns of feelings arising from varied situations. Literature gives form and content.

From their general experience of stories and poems children are enabled to satisfy what Wallace Stevens in 'The Idea of Order at Key West' calls 'our blessed rage for order'. However, particular stories seem to meet children's need for security and reassurance in singular and intense ways. In 'The Peppermint Lesson', Moss (1977) records how a deep and sustaining bond was established between her adopted daughter's emotional need and an ostensibly unremarkable tale about a kitten called Peppermint. Beneath the rather mawkish surface of the tale her daughter Alison had obviously found a moving image of her own predicament. Such a book, Moss contends, may, if the emotional content is sound, 'hold a message of supreme significance for a particular child' and if it does 'will be more important to that child's development than all the Kate Greenaway award-winning books put together'. Similarly in *Cushla and Her Books* Butler (1979) gives us a detailed and moving account of how books provided for her handicapped granddaughter not only the security that comes from a developing sense of self and knowledge of the world, but also a massive enrichment of her life that 'contributed enormously to her cognitive development in general and her language in particular'. That the 'eager ingestion' of books 'helps such children to find meaning in the complex and contradictory experiences of life' is for Butler 'self-evident'. And to the extent that children with special needs are likely to be, though are not of course necessarily, more subject to a disharmonious and puzzling world, it could be argued that they are more likely to need literature's propensity for holding, shaping and illuminating human experience. Also, as Warnock (1978) points out, children who are disturbed in feeling or behaviour can especially benefit from an enrichment of language that gives greater scope to their own expressive needs.

Hardy (1968), indicating the importance of narrative to the satisfaction of that need, writes: 'We dream in narrative, day-dream in narrative, remember, anticipate, hope, despair, believe, doubt, plan, revise, criticize, construct, gossip, learn, hate and love by narrative.' Narrative, she suggests is a 'primary act of the mind transferred from life to art'. Ted Hughes (1970) makes a similar point, describing stories as 'little factories of understanding' that children take possession of as 'units of imagination' and that offer 'the beginning of imaginative and mental control … the beginning of a form of contemplation'.

Ted Hughes' belief in the power of story, and especially myths and fables, to mediate between the outer world of external reality and the inner world of the child's thoughts and feelings, and to shape into significance and graspable order the often amorphous or fleeting elements of day-to-day living – you cannot live and tell, as Antoine Roquentin in Sartre's *Nausea* avers – is endorsed by Bettelheim (1976). He claims fairy tales as a healing medium in his work as an educator and therapist of severely disturbed children. For Bettelheim the most pressing need that people have and 'the most difficult of achievement' is 'to find meaning in their lives'; and he believes that fairy tales 'speak about severe inner pressures in a way that the child unconsciously understands', and that without 'belittling the most serious inner struggles which growing up entails offer examples of both temporary and permanent solutions to pressing difficulties'.

The search for meaning, however, can operate at less intense levels, and it is interesting to note that in the experiment undertaken by Hughes (in Donaldson, 1978), which showed that children were far more competent at imaginative 'decentring' than Piaget had believed, what the children were faced with was basically a narrative situation: a policeman searching for children in hiding. Hughes' experiment endorses the point made by Moffett (1968) that: 'whereas adults differentiate their thoughts into specialized kinds of discourse such as narrative, generalizations and theory, children for a long time make narrative do for all'.

For Rosen (1983) narrative is a basic grammar of the mind whereby children are aided to confirm, or extend their felt understanding of the world, to interpret their experience in the light of what they read, and to evaluate what they read in the light of their increasing knowledge in that fructifying interchange of life and literature that informs reading at its most rewarding. His affirmation of the continuing value of story has clear implications for the provision of literature in school:

> We might be disposed to take stories more seriously if we perceived them first and foremost as a product of the human mind to narratize experience and to transform it into findings which as social beings we may share and compare with those of others.

ANSWERING THE NEED FOR PRAISE AND RECOGNITION

Ironically, reading for children is so often not intrinsically rewarding that it becomes a potent source of disappointment and frustration, the means whereby children are demeaned and devalued in their own eyes and lose that notion of self-esteem that is essential to the satisfaction of Kellmer Pringle's third major need: praise and recognition. The sense of pleasure and achievement that comes from an enjoyed book brings with it a satisfaction that endorses the activity of reading; but what could be more corrosive of self-esteem for a young child than to be debarred from or frustrated by a process that is so highly and universally valued?

Recent work by adults on basic literacy schemes bears powerful testimony to the deeply debilitating long-term effects, the damage to both person and prospects, when reading is not mastered at school (Gatehouse, 1984). Literature, of itself, cannot confer upon the reader praise or recognition: but if the pleasure that literature gives can be made an essential element of children's engagements with books from the outset, we can hope to have fewer readers who are thwarted or defeated in the process.

ANSWERING THE NEED FOR RESPONSIBILITY

What of Kellmer Pringle's fourth need, responsibility? On the face of it, it might seem to have no connection with literature whatsoever. We normally think of responsibilities as duties or obligations that have to be carried out fully and conscientiously. The reader absorbed in a book, filling his or her head with fictions while the necessary tasks of the everyday world remain uncompleted, might be seen as the very emblem of an irresponsible person. In engaging with a fiction, however, the reader may be facing responsibilities, or rather beginning to realise what responsibility entails, by an imaginative involvement in fictional worlds that explore and vivify the complexities of our being in the world, with all its attendant paradoxes and ironies, its possibilities and its dilemmas. 'Art, and especially literature', Murdoch (1977) reminds us, 'is a great hall of reflection where we can all meet and where everything under the sun can be examined and considered.' 'Imagining reality the better to test it' (Jones, 1968) provides the child with special needs, as well as the adult, with a secondary world where perspectives on life as it is and life as it might be can be gained.

In this sense literature becomes, in Harding's (1962) words, 'an accepted technique for viewing the chances of life'. In the evaluative response of the reader to the text are possibilities of reflection and refinement of judgement of a kind that distinguish informed, responsible actions. 'We had the experience but missed the meaning' writes T. S. Eliot in *Four Quartets*, a point that Harding (op.

cit.), drawing the parallel between onlooker and reader, elaborates thus:

> They [i.e. the events we merely witness] may in certain ways be even more formative than events in which we take part. Detached and distanced evaluation is sometimes sharper for avoiding the blurrings and buffetings that participant action brings, and the spectator often sees the events in a broader context than participant can tolerate. To obliterate the effects on a man of the occasions on which he was only an onlooker would be profoundly to change his outlook and values.

Literature allows us to look on at a range of experiences that an ordinary life would not otherwise share. It can reassure, and it can profoundly challenge. W. B. Yeats prefaced a collection of poems entitled *Responsibilities* with the epigraph, 'In dreams begins responsibility', aware that in the liberated order of art the highest potentialities of our incomplete humanity might be discerned.

INTRODUCING LITERATURE

For children with special needs to benefit from literature they must, of course, have access to it, they must, quite simply, be willing readers, eager for and receptive to the intellectual and emotional sustenance that it proffers.

The kind of readers we produce, however, will depend to a great extent on their initial school experience of learning to read. There is a growing body of theory and research that stresses the importance of 'powerful narrative forms as the most suitable diet for novice readers' (Moon, 1984). This emphasis stems from the work of, among others, Huey (1908), Smith (1971), the Goodmans (1982) and Meek (1982), who have demonstrated the need to see reading within an overall pattern of language development. They show it as a part of children's continuing quest to make sense of the world, akin to their acquisition of spoken language, and mastered primarily not by the accumulation of an armoury of sub-skills, but by their desire to understand what they deem useful and worthy of understanding. Of vital importance to the implementation of this view of reading is the provision of stories which, though appropriate to the experience and ability of the child reader, have, none the less, qualities that appeal to both mind and heart, that speak with the energy of crafted language to children's love of fun, their uncertainty in the face of what they find strange and threatening, and their innate drive to order what Robert Graves in 'Warning to Children' has called the 'richness, muchness, strangeness' of the world in which they find themselves. Reading, it is suggested, can be made a natural, enjoyable process that child and adult share, not an anxiety-inducing rite that, even where it succeeds, leaves so many readers able but unwilling to turn to books for either pleasure or profit.

There are numerous studies of the advantages to pre-school children of a shared experience of books and stories (Clark, 1976; Butler, 1979; Hewison, 1979) and there is growing evidence of the effectiveness of the theory in terms of classroom practice at all levels (Huck, 1979; Ousby, 1980; Bennet, 1982; Meek, 1983; Walsh, 1983; Graham, 1984; Williams, 1985). Waterland's *Read with Me* (1985) is the most detailed account to date of the practicalities of a story-centred approach to the teaching of reading, and she is in no doubt that the theory works in practice. She asserts:

> Children of eight and nine classed once as 'failed' or remedial readers can no longer fail. Many have had satisfying experiences for the first time in their lives, they have discovered that reading books is good and they can do it.

Enthusiastic proponents of a particular method are not a guarantee of its success, but Waterland's 'apprenticeship approach' to reading has positive implications for the provision of literature to children with special needs. By its emphasis on reading as a natural extension of the child's growing mastery of language it avoids the deficit model that so often sees the child as someone who is failing the learning system rather than vice versa. The primacy it gives to enjoyable texts as a crucial means of motivating children to want to read, commonsense and experience endorse. (The writer heard recently of a boy who attempted to inject some life into his graded reader by reading it from back to front!) It respects the language the children already possess and invites them to behave from the beginning as readers of books rather than readers of what Huey (1908) called the 'sentence-hash of primers'. In its eschewing of skills practised in isolation it rescues the child from the paradoxical situation whereby 'children who do not learn to read easily are often expected to learn in the most difficult way possible' (Smith, 1978).

Moyle (1982), stressing the importance of stories as one of the key ways into reading, writes: 'The essential point is that if we are to overcome any lag in development or difficulty a child has, it becomes even more important that the work given emphasises the reality, usefulness and enjoyment of language activities.' The downward destructive spiral of failure creating anxiety, and anxiety causing failure is probably the greatest hurdle, apart from some of the most extreme forms of learning difficulties, that a child has to overcome. Compared with the inner paralysis of being that anxiety creates, physical disabilities may appear relatively minor obstacles. Wade and Moore's (1987) case study of 8-year-old Dean, an 'extreme case of reading difficulty', exemplifies this point clearly. Physically he was a normal child, but his failure to learn to read was a source of deep emotional distress to him. Clearly, attempting to teach him to read using the methods that had already failed would only stigmatise his failure even more deeply. Instead, an apprenticeship approach was adopted. His teacher shared with him a wide range of real books (the importance of picture books in this kind of situation is manifest). One of them – *My Cat Likes to hide in Boxes* by Eve Sutton – emerged as a clear favourite, and eventually, through a process of paired reading, Dean was enabled to read it and, crucially, experience reading as something rewarding and satisfying. This radical shift in the boy's outlook marked the beginning of his tentative progress as a reader.

MOTIVATING THE READING OF LITERATURE

Literature, then, has a key rôle to play in the creation of readers. It can also help to win back to more purposeful and rewarding reading those disaffected children who seem to share the same attitude as the boy in Southgate's (1981) study who when asked why he should learn to read, replied 'So then we can stop.' Meek (1983) leaves us in no doubt of the difficulties that teachers face when a distrust of books has become deeply ingrained, but she also demonstrates the efficacy of a commitment to literature in leading 'failed' children back to the pleasures that reading offers. Williams (1985) describes how the fun and value of reading was made available to a group of 13 children in a special education class by an approach that placed a major emphasis on 'narrative texts, the children's own narratives and others published for them'. Huck (1979) describes improvements in attitudes to reading that were consequent upon a similar provision of narrative texts with slower learners. In this instance, a school that was determined on improving the children's involvement with books decided against employing a remedial teacher and instead employed a teacher who 'could turn children on to reading, particularly those children who could read but who didn't'. The 'reading motivator', as she was called, initiated a programme in which: all the teachers read to their children every day; there was a sustained silent reading period every afternoon during which teachers read books recommended by the children; sets of four or five paperbacks of the same title were bought for children to read together, discuss and interpret through games, drama, personal writing, etc.; and parent aides helped children bind their own books, which were then made available for everyone to read. Not only were test scores improved, but more importantly they 'discovered that children would read when they found pleasure in reading'.

Fry (1985), in his taped conversations with 8-year-old Clayton, sensitively charts how the boy, by a very challenging but rewarding engagement with *Watership Down*, moved from the view that stories were merely light diversion rather than part of the serious business of living to an awareness that literature offers what Rosenblatt (1970) describes as a 'seeing for yourself, a living through not simply knowledge about'. Crucially instrumental in this development was the class teacher who believed that because books and story telling were central to her teaching Clayton would learn to value them in his own time and for his own reasons. Also worthy of note here are the various ways in which the boy was allowed 'the opportunity to experience the story in different ways, and to work out the experience through a variety of forms'. These included: showing other children his picture book and telling them the story; recording on tape conversations he had about the book with his teacher and other adults; making an advertisement for the film-of-the-book; telling the story to the class in preparation for drama; acting out the story and playing the part of a character; asking questions about the book in a letter to the author, in a letter to another adult, on tape to his teacher; at home, having the story read aloud, and reading to himself.

THE RÔLE OF THE TEACHER

The wise patience that facilitated Clayton's realisation of the value of reading is a pertinent reminder that it is the teacher who is best placed to recognise the needs of individual children. Informing any practical steps that the teacher might take, however, should be the crucial awareness that we cannot really teach literature at all. A story is something we experience and bring into being as individuals; no one can have the experience for us. If a work of literature does not speak to us personally, if our knowledge of life and literature is such that words on the page do not come alive, we are unlikely to value that work no matter how vehemently we are exhorted to by others. This is not to say that our initial response to a work may not be altered by discussion or by the more intimate acquaintance that results from the active exploration of poems, stories and plays in performance. The child's initial response, however, must be respected. Approaches to literature that disregard this principle, that pre-package what the children's responses will be and ignore the essentially personal nature of our responses to imaginative works, deny the collaborative creativity of reader and text. Stories and poems are often used in the most arid kind of comprehension exercises, and children are given the impression that literature is a puzzle to which there are set answers. Children are also made to feel culpable for their inability to admire and enjoy recommended works, especially those canonised with the label of 'classic'. Such practice is not conducive to the creation of confident readers, and certainly with young children with special needs and those who are distrustful of reading it is likely to prove most harmful. With this caveat in mind, approaches to literature in the classroom can now be considered.

The teacher's rôle will, of course, be vital. Ample provision of a wide range of books, attractive display, congenial reading areas, will have little more than cosmetic appeal if the teacher does not convey to the class her own enthusiasm for and love of books. Most obviously the teacher who wishes to share her commitment to the value of literature will be someone who is knowledgeable about books, who expresses an interest in the books the children are reading, who is seen to be a keen reader. Shapiro (1979) argues persuasively that teacher attitudes play an influential rôle in determining children's views of reading, and he stresses that often children receive contradictory messages: the teacher may explicitly tell children that reading is important, but his or her non-verbal behaviour may, in fact, totally negate this. The same can be true of the school as a whole. The book corners of many primary classrooms do not always suggest 'a vibrant interest in good children's literature' (Anning, 1987). Moreover, where schools isolate story time to a short period at the end of the afternoon when the 'real' business of the school day is over, they are implicitly devaluing it.

READING ALOUD

Frequent reading aloud from a wide diversity of texts is the teacher's most effective means for making the pleasures of literature available to the greatest number of children. An expressive performance, for the appropriate age-level, of such tried and tested favourites as *The Great Big Enormous Turnip* by Alexei Tolstoy, *Burglar Bill* by Janet and Allan Ahlberg, *How Tom Beat Captain Najork and His Hired Sportsmen* by Russell Hoban, *The Owl Who Was Afraid of the Dark* by Jill Tomlinson, *Charlotte's Web* by E. B. White, *How the Whale Became and Other Stories* by Ted Hughes, the excellent collection *Our Best Stories* by Anne Wood and Anne Pilling, and *The Eighteenth Emergency* by Betsy Byars, will not only serve as an appetiser for the children, but also enable them to 'become increasingly familiar with the language of books and better able to recognise the patterns of written text in the books they read for themselves' (Wells, 1981).

For Bennett (1982) reading aloud by the teacher from real books constitutes the essential experience from which the development of reading and dedicated readers follow. Her personal conviction is supported by the research of Wells (op. cit.) and by American research, which indicates the following benefits to children of hearing stories read aloud: the child gains an overall insight into the nature of books and what it means to be a reader; it is the means whereby children achieve the essential realisation that print has meaning; the shared experience of story with a respected adult is instrumental in giving the child a sense of the value of books; children learn about the form and structure of the written language; significant gains in vocabulary are acquired (Teale, 1984). Also, as Donaldson (1982) points out, the expressive use of gesture, intonation, facial expression and so on, can, when employed by a skilled reader or storyteller, make accessible to the children narratives that they would not be capable of reading on their own. Because of this, she argues, teachers should, occasionally, make use of a 'calculated disparity' between the texts the children are able to read unaided and those the teacher reads aloud to them. As children grow older they will meet stories of increasing linguistic complexity and will continue to need the helpful familiarisation that listening to texts provides. The tendency to read aloud less to older children ignores this important aspect of hearing stories read. And, of course, a greater familiarisation with the nature of written language has far-reaching consequences for the development of expressive writing skills.

TALKING ABOUT LITERATURE

Talk tends to be our spontaneous reaction to most human experiences, including literature, and children should be given frequent opportunities to discuss the stories they listen to. This most natural of responses needs to be nurtured and encouraged if children are to sense that their reactions to a story have value and importance for others. Reflections on the characters, anticipation of likely developments, relating the events of the story to their own lives – all these activities allow children to re-explore the story, to find their own distinctive ways of saying what it means to them without any feeling of coercion or of searching for pre-determined answers. Young children are invariably highly anecdotal in their responses and on occasions the story may seem to be little more than a springboard for a variety of personal reminiscences. This, especially with primary school children, is perfectly acceptable and, indeed, is usually part of discussion of literature at any level. However, if literature were nothing more than a lively prompt for personal memories and other activities it would hardly warrant a major place in the curriculum, a point we will return to later. Once an atmosphere of mutual trust and respect has been established, and as the quality of children's reflections mature and develop, the teacher will be able to draw upon their reading to enable her pupils to gain a more confident perspective on their own experience, (Have you been frightened, like Frances, of going to bed?); to invite them into imaginative speculations (What do you think would happen if you used a toothpaste that made you tell the truth all the time?); to challenge stereotyped views (What made you so sure Tyke Tyler was a boy?); to prompt ethical considerations (Would you want to go to a school where the headmaster hypnotized the pupils?); and to provide opportunities for sympathetic identification (If you had been in a family that had accepted evacuees like Willy Beech how would you have felt?). Oral work of this kind not only allows children to express their thoughts and feelings, but also gives them the opportunity in a supportive context of exploring and becoming familiar with the language structures of speculation and reflection. Also, and this is of paramount importance, it is in this activity that children learn to use language in a way that has important consequences for later learning. In this activity, as Wells (1985) points out, the child learns:

> to disembed his thinking from the context of immediate activity ... and operate upon experience, both real and hypothetical, through the medium of words alone. Stories, and the talk that arises from them, provide an important introduction to this intellectually powerful function of language.

Discussion is important for another reason. Readers tend to create fiction in their own image. Purves and Beach (1972) and Holland (1975) have shown the extent to which stories are moulded by the personalities and predilections of individual readers. Discussion can provide a necessary corrective viewpoint to our own limited responses. Blake's couplet

> You read the Bible day and night
> But I read black where you read white.

makes the same point very tellingly.

Just how sensitively and perceptively children can respond in discussion to their reading when they are accorded the status of responsive readers is illustrated in the detailed conversations recorded by Fry (1985). Admittedly, Fry, as a researcher, was not subjected to the demanding pressures of a primary classroom. However, Paley's (1981) remarkable book *Wally's Stories* demonstrates most persuasively the extent to which a committed teacher can use stories as a key source for stimulating and vivifying a varied spectrum of curriculum activities. Her day-by-day tape recordings show that for her pupils stories are not only enjoyable experiences in themselves but also a wellspring of exploratory talk, of speculation, of hypothesising, of interpretation, a means of making sense of the world and the children's relationships within it: young as they are, they have entered, at a level appropriate to themselves, 'that great hall of reflection ... where everything under the sun can be considered' (Murdoch, 1977).

WORKING TOGETHER

Group work of various kinds can be especially helpful in making involvement with literature enjoyable. Vygotsky's (1962) contention that what the child can do today in co-operation tomorrow he will be able to do alone is especially relevant here. For many disillusioned readers literature is a closed world, and in order to make it accessible we need to demystify books in very positive ways. Shared writing, where the class and teacher, or children in small groups, collaborate to produce their own story is one such practice that offers the child the chance to create and have control over that which formerly appeared remote or forbidding. If the book that is then produced is accorded the same importance that attaches to those professionally produced (given permanent form, read to the class, discussed, added to the class library, read to younger children) both worth and status are conferred on the authors. Graves (1983) found that when teachers read work produced by children and stories by established authors in the same session, and treated them both in the same manner, 'the children's concept of authority changed dramatically and increased confidence in both the assessment and production of stories resulted'.

WORKING ALONE

Eventually, of course, we are intent upon creating independent readers who will need ample time for private reading. Southgate

(1981) found that there was a tendency for teachers to allow insufficient time for this activity, and an assumption that once children have learned to read a close interest in their voluntary reading by the teacher is no longer necessary.

Given the numerous distractions that many children face at home it is imperative that schools demonstrate their commitment to reading by providing time for it in the curriculum. And if teachers are to help the hesitant reader in the long journey to independent enjoyment of literature they will need to take a continuing and active interest in all aspects of their pupils' reading.

Parents also have an important rôle to play. Parental involvement, which has been a more common feature of special rather than of mainstream education, can clearly be of benefit to all children. The effectiveness of parents in the teaching of reading is now well established, and their participation in this process should go hand in hand with the promotion of the appeal of literature. The apprenticeship approach, referred to earlier, which has much in common with the successful paired reading schemes documented in Topping and Wolfendale (1985), can profit from the involvement of parents as both readers and listeners. The initiatives described by Obrist (1984) in alerting the parents of pre-school children to the need for early provision of books – the setting up of the Federation of Children's Book Groups, family reading groups and toddlers' reading clubs – are all to be welcomed; and her suggestion that adolescents on parenthood courses in secondary schools should be fully apprised of the ways in which the pleasurable experience of books can aid a child's education merits widespread implementation.

INVOLVING THE PARENTS

Links with home can also provide invaluable insights into the sources of problems that arise in school. When contact with Dean's home (Wade and Moore, 1987) was made it was discovered that when the boy read to his parents they laughed at his mistakes. Such an incident reminds us very forcibly of the need for liaison between the school and the home and the difficulties that might be encountered when it is attempted. However, when there is energetic commitment to parental involvement successful schemes such as the CAPER (Children and Parents Enjoying Reading) and PACT (Parents and Children and Teachers) projects can result, and offer useful models of a 'parent friendly' approach, and ones in which due attention is paid to the content of what children read as well as parent skills (Griffiths and Hamilton, 1984; Branston and

Provis, 1986). That such schemes need wide support is suggested by Hannon and Cuckle (1984) who, in a small-scale survey of 16 infant and first schools found that though books were sent home parents were not given any specific guidance about helping their children with reading.

Where good working relationships have been set-up more ambitious undertakings can be effected. Research carried out by Wade (1984) is particularly relevant here. It was posited on the crucial importance of real stories as source material and set out to discover if children's propensity for 'storying' – i.e. the ability to shape and order into narrative their personal experience of both life and fiction –'depended solely on steadily maturing skills or whether they could be speeded up by enlisting parental cooperation with school'. In fact, significant gains were made by the experimental group who, during the period of the research, had stories read to them on a regular basis by the parents, and, in turn, told stories to their parents. Although the research was not carried out with children with special needs, it seems reasonable to infer that similar gains would be possible for them. Ellis (1985) believes that,

> The 'storying' which allows younger and older children to speculate and hypothesise, to reshape past events and organise present experience has often been insufficiently recognised and developed for groups with learning difficulties, indeed, the difficulties may well have arisen through insufficient nurturing of this process at school.

Improvements in children's ability to manipulate narrative techniques are clearly to be welcomed. There is a danger, however, as we noted earlier, that literature can come to be used in the curriculum as a mere servicing of other subjects. At its most insensitive this approach is exemplified by the person who asks of a children's author 'Can you tell me about a novel to do with rain?' or 'Can you tell me about a novel I can use in a project on the police force?' (Chambers, 1986). Seen thus, literature is simply curiously packaged information, to be raided at will for whatever facts are relevant to the theme in hand. Used in this way it would hardly warrant the central rôle in the primary curriculum which, by implication, we have been suggesting it should have. For that to be the case, its full creative potential needs to be acknowledged.

CREATIVE RESPONSES

Where children's engagement with literature is particularly intense or playful, the imaginative charge generated often seems to seek outlets in creative expression of various kinds. Such expression (play-making, movement, painting, story or poetry writing) is creative in the usual sense of the word in that by the exercise of the imagination something new is brought into being. In the creation of these imaginative works children are attempting to draw on the resources of a particular medium to give heightened expression to their thoughts and feelings. The process, however, is not simply one of giving expression to something already clear and complete: creative activities of this kind are often a means whereby we discover what our thoughts and feelings actually are.

There is another area of creativity to which literature, less obviously, makes a vital contribution. Elliot (1971), in an illuminating essay, points out that the decline in belief in a divine creator has led to a new emphasis on a concept of creativity that stresses self-creation, the bringing of ourselves into being. Lying behind this concept is Nietzsche's 'understanding of creativeness as the overcoming of what our world seeks to impose on us as necessity'. Such considerations may appear remote from literature and the needs of children in primary classrooms, but such a notion would be mistaken. For example, the child who reads *I Can Jump Puddles* by Alan Marshall has access to powerful and liberating insights; by depicting most feelingly how he coped with poliomyelitis Marshall reveals how he overcame what the world 'tried to impose on him as necessity' and in so doing illustrates and challenges the stereotyped view of handicap that the world seeks to impose upon us. Literature at its most powerful has this potential for undermining our limited and partial views; it opens up new worlds, new possibilities. Children with special needs will vary enormously in their abilities, in the extent to which they can inhabit those worlds, entertain those possibilities, but we must strive to ensure that no one is debarred.

POETRY AND THE NURTURING OF A LOVE OF LANGUAGE

Integral to that endeavour will be a desire to promote in children an alertness to the appeal of language in all its manifold aspects, and it is here, particularly, that poetry can make a vital contribution. For it to make that contribution, however, there will need to be a fundamental change from the situation that obtains currently. Benton's (1978) claim that 'handling poetry is the area of primary/middle school curriculum ... where teachers feel most uncertain of their knowledge, most uncomfortable about their methods, and most guilty about both' is a valid one, and he is justified in referring to poetry as a 'neglected art'. The reasons for this are numerous (cf. Benton, op. cit.; Fitzpatrick, 1986), but the outcome is that too often poetry is accorded little time or status in the curriculum, a subject that, like music and art, must give way to the more pressing demands of the much vaunted 'basics'. There is a false reasoning at work here. A narrow emphasis on basics can often stultify the very skills it is intended to cultivate. It would seem axiomatic that a sense of delight in language itself will have beneficial consequences for all aspects of language use, and, in fact, the majority of young children, as they come to consciousness of their possession of this invaluable gift, do take a spontaneous pleasure in it. The work of Chukovsky (1963) and the Opies (1959) bears abundant testimony to children's love of rhythm and rhyme, of jokes, puns, alliteration and word play of various kinds. When children designate the school nurse as

Nitty Nora
The bug explorer

they are exercising their natural propensity for rhythm and rhyme, for alliteration, for comic possibilities of sound, and the deflationary effects of such startling verbal collisions as 'bug explorer'. By playing with these elements children gain mastery of them.

Unfortunately, play is still not accorded by schools its rightful and potent rôle in the development of children's language: the mechanical exercises persistently censured by HMI reports are indicative of an overall impoverished provision that is still far too prevalent and in which poetry has little or no place. And yet poetry offers the most obvious way of sustaining, nurturing and eventually refining a child's love of language, by extending and developing those very qualities of the medium to which children are so powerfully attracted. That attraction can be the first step towards later mastery. Dylan Thomas (1966) records how a lifelong fascination began with the rhymes of infancy:

> The first poems I knew were nursery rhymes, and before I could read them myself I had come to love just the words of them, the words alone. What the words stood for, symbolized, or meant, was of secondary importance.

Similarly, Seamus Heaney (1980) recalls his childhood delight in the crude rhymes of the playground, and the magical and mysterious names of the shipping forecast: Dogger, Rockall, Malin, Shetland, Faroes, Finisterre ... As Wade (1982), in an illuminating account of the importance of poetry for young children, comments: 'His [Heaney's] account is valuable in suggesting that childhood contacts with arresting, imaginative words and the maturely organized verse of the poet are part of the same continuum.'

Of course, poetry is not simply the jokes, the jingles, the catchy rhymes, the nonsense, the phonic fun of nursery rhymes. It speaks to children's needs in more serious ways. At its most effective and affective, it employs all the resources of language to create in the reader feeling insights into a diverse array of human experiences. No single group of children has a monopoly on feeling, and the powerful fusion of emotion and highly-charged rhythmical language characteristic of poetry makes available to all children in a condensed and heightened form what Louis MacNeice in 'Snow' calls the 'incorrigible plurality' of the world, 'the drunkenness of things being various'.

In approaching poetry in the classroom it is essential, as indeed with all our dealings with literature, that we keep the primacy of pleasure clearly in view. Excellent models have been provided, not surprisingly, by poets themselves (Ted Hughes, 1967; Kenneth Koch, 1974) and a number of recent publications offer excellent guiding principles and useful suggestions for practice (Brownjohn, 1980, 1982; Calthrop and Ede, 1984; Benton and Fox, 1985; Corbett and Moses, 1986).

Bringing poets into schools especially recommends itself as a way of providing working examples to both teachers and pupils of those practitioners who respect language and are highly skilled in its use. The following poems must stand as representative of a rich body of work written by children working with the poet Gillian Clarke (in Howells (n.d.)).

A Waterfall
As I walk I see the Waterfall,
It is sometimes angry and frightening,
Jumping from the dull shadowy rocks,
Down into a pool of white foam.
It sometimes is happy,
Dancing as if it were in Heaven,
Where people dance in colourful fields of green,
Sometimes, it daydreams,
Shouting out strange things.

Sian

The Countryside
As we walked through the sunny countryside,
The pink blossoms fell one by one.
The orchards full of fruit ripening everywhere,
All like a new world just begun.
The squirrels jumping merrily to and fro,

The birds singing their beautiful songs,
The green grass freshly cut,
And the old oak tree bushing out.

Darren

OVERCOMING THE OBSTACLES

Ample provision of language as play is vital for all, but especially necessary to supplement the work of those children whose difficulties with language appear to necessitate structured programmes that are not intrinsically appealing to the child. Literature, we have suggested, has an especial contribution to make, not only because it speaks to the major needs outlined by Kellmer Pringle and thereby becomes a formative agent of emotional and intellectual growth, but also because its distinctive nurturing of an awareness and love of language in all its forms has far-reaching implications for every aspect of a child's education. But to what extent is the enrichment that literature offers available to all? As more children with special needs are integrated into mainstream schools, what particular obstacles will need to be overcome? The first point to be stressed, obviously, is that many disabilities do not in themselves constitute a barrier to the enjoyment of literature. In partially-sighted, hearing-impaired, or cerebral palsied children, for example, there may be considerable difficulties of access, but, without in any way minimising these, they are not insurmountable. The catalogue of library holdings published by The National Library for the Handicapped Child (1986) provides a useful guide to the extensive range of resources that are now available.

Equally, emotional and behavioural problems are not, necessarily, impediments to an engagement with literature. Indeed, books can be a powerful source of comfort and reassurance at times of isolation and stress, as numerous autobiographies make clear. Moreover, insight into problems can be afforded by the discussions that arise from the reading of a poem or a story. As Wilson (1983), reflecting on the findings of a Schools Council Project on the education of children with special needs comments:

> We noted ... that children could often express themselves more freely and show more insight in discussing the problems of other people than in speaking of their own. Stories offer many situations and characters which can stimulate such discussions. Inevitably some children will see relevance to their own problems even if they do not admit this openly.

Wilson also makes the interesting point that 'without doubt some children not given to kindness, have had their tenderness and sympathy aroused by fiction'. A point that recalls both Kafka's belief that books should be like axes to break the frozen seas of ice within us and Shelley's claim in *A Defence of Poetry* that

> A man, to be greatly good, must imagine intensely and comprehensively, he must put himself in the place of another and of many others; the pains and pleasures of the species must become his own. The great instrument of moral good is the imagination; and poetry administers to the effect by acting upon the cause.

Greater difficulties may arise when children are subject to severe learning difficulties. What can be achieved in extreme cases (cf. Butler, 1979; Anderson, 1985) by dedicated and committed parents should serve as an inspirational reminder to us as teachers, however, and make us hesitate to limit the lives of those we teach by the inadequacy of our expectations.

Expectations, of course, our own and our pupils', are often determined by assumptions and prejudices. That these can be challenged and altered by reading experiences has been shown in connection with children's attitudes to ethnic minorities, in research reviewed by Campbell and Wirtenberg (1980). Reference has already been made to Alan Marshall's *I Can Jump Puddles* and Ivan Southall's *Let The Balloon Go* as books (for older juniors) that offer vivid depictions into the lives of the disabled and may be instrumental in prompting greater understanding. The depiction of disability in recent fiction for children as well as a discussion of what approaches to it in the classroom are likely to be most successful is explored very sensitively in Quicke's (1985) *Disability in Modern Children's Fiction*. Though predominantly concerned with the secondary school age range, this book has a chapter on books for the primary school level and offers much that will be of interest to all concerned with literature and special needs.

At the simplest level of engagement literature offers to children a lifelong source of pleasure. When experienced pleasurably it speaks to children's fundamental needs. At its most powerful 'it states and considers alternative possible realities – allowing escape from the prison of current fact' (Gregory, 1977), and it is for that reason, as Bruner (1986) notes, that 'tyrants so hate and fear poets and novelists'.

Many children in our schools are held in 'the prison of current fact', and for some children with special needs the limits of the prison are particularly constricting. It is our task as teachers to make available to them that mode of imaginative thinking where, in

Seamus Heaney's (1986) words: 'We go beyond our normal cognitive bounds and sense a new element where we are not alien but liberated, more alive to ourselves, more drawn out, more educated'.

REFERENCES

Anderson, R. (1985) Books for the special child. *Signal* (47).
Anning, A. (1987) Hanging on in there. *Times Educational Supplement* 20 March.
Bennett, J. (1982) 'Learning to read with real books', In M. Hoffman, R. Jeffcoate, J. Maybin and N. Mercer (eds) *Children, Language and Literature.* Open University Inset P 530 CB. Milton Keynes: Open University Press.
Benton, M. (1978) Poetry for children: a neglected art. *Children's Literature in Education* 9 (3).
Benton, M. and Fox, G. (1985) *Teaching Literature: Nine to Fourteen.* Oxford: Oxford University Press.
Bettelheim, B. (1976) *The Uses of Enchantment.* London: Thames and Hudson.
Branston, P. and Provis, M. (1986) *Children and Parents Enjoying Reading.* London: Hodder and Stoughton.
Brownjohn, S. (1980) *Does it Have to Rhyme?* London: Hodder and Stoughton.
Brownjohn, S. (1982) *What Rhymes with Secret?* London: Hodder and Stoughton.
Bruner, J. (1986) *Actual Minds, Possible Worlds.* London: Harvard University Press.
Butler, D. (1979) *Cushla and Her Books.* London: Hodder and Stoughton.
Calthrop, K. and Ede, J. (eds) (1984) *Not 'Daffodils' Again: Teaching Poetry 9–13.* Schools Council Programme 2. London: Longman.
Campbell, P. B. and Wirtenberg, J. (1980) How books influence children: what the research shows. *International Books for Children Bulletin,* **11** (6).
Chambers, A. (1986) Booktalk: an interview with Aidan Chambers. *The English Magazine* (17).
Chukovsky, K. (1963) *From Two to Five* (trans. Miriam Morton). Berkeley: University of California Press.
Clark, M. (1976) *Young Fluent Readers.* London: Heinemann Educational.
Corbett, P. and Moses, B. (1986) *Catapults and Kingfishers: Teaching Poetry in Primary Schools.* Oxford: Oxford University Press.
Croll, P. and Moses, D. (1985) *One in Five: The Assessment and Incidence of Special Educational Needs.* London: Routledge & Kegan Paul.
Daiches, D. (1956) *Critical Approaches to Literature.* London: Longman.
Donaldson, M. (1978) *Children's Minds.* London: Fontana.
Donaldson, M. (1982) 'Literature and language development'. In M. Hoffman, R. Jeffcoate, J. Maybin and N. Mercer (eds) *Children, Language and Literature.* Open University Inset P530 CB, Milton Keynes: Open University Press.

Elliot, R. K. (1971) Versions of creativity. *Proceedings of the Philosophy of Education Society of Great Britain* 5 (2).

Ellis, J. (1985) Enriching the curriculum through literature. *British Journal of Special Education* 12 (2).

Fischer, E. (1963) *The Necessity of Art*. Harmondsworth: Penguin.

Fitzpatrick, J. (1986) Literature in the primary school: pitfalls and possibilities. *Primary Contact* 4 (1).

Frost, R. (1939) Preface to *Collected Poems*. New York: Holt, Rinehart and Winston.

Fry, D. (1985) *Children Talk About Books: Seeing Themselves as Readers*. Milton Keynes: Open University Press.

Gatehouse (1984) *Where Do We Go from Here?* Manchester: Gatehouse Project.

Goodman, K., S. and Yetta, M. (1982) *Language and Literacy: The Selected Writings of Kenneth S. Goodman*. Vols I and II, London: Routledge & Kegan Paul.

Graham, J. (1984) 'Reading literature with a slow learner'. In J. Miller (ed.) *Eccentric Propositions*. London: Routledge & Kegan Paul.

Graves, D. (1983) *Writing: Teachers and Children at Work*. London: Heinemann Educational.

Gregory, R. L. (1977) 'Psychology: towards a science of fiction'. In M. Meek, A. Warlow and G. Barton (eds) *The Cool Web*. London: Bodley Head.

Griffiths, A. and Hamilton, D. (1984) *Parent, Teacher, Child*. London: Methuen.

Hannon, P. W. and Cuckle, P. (1984) Involving parents in the teaching of reading: study of current school practice. *Education Research* 26 (1).

Harding, D. W. (1962) Psychological processes in the reading of fiction. *British Journal of Aesthetics* 2.

Hardy, B. (1968) Towards a poetics of fiction: an approach through narrative. *Novel: A Forum on Fiction* 2 (1).

Heaney, S. (1980) *Preoccupations: Selected Prose 1968–1978*. London: Faber.

Heaney, S. (1986) Among schoolchildren. *Signal* (47).

Heeks, P. (1981) *Choosing and Using Books in the First School*. London: Macmillan.

Hewison, J. (1979) 'Home environment and reading attainment: a study of children in a working class community'. PhD thesis, University of London.

Holland, N. (1975) *Five Readers Reading*. New Haven: Yale University Press.

Howells, B. (ed.) (n.d.) 'The Patchwork Quilt: An Anthology of Children's Poems'. Unpublished. Durham Road Junior School, Durham Road, Newport, Gwent.

Huck, C. (1979) 'No wider than the heart is wide'. In J. E. Shapiro (ed.) *Using Literature Affectively*. Newark: International Reading Association.

Huey, E. G. (1908) *The Psychology and Pedagogy of Reading*. Reprinted in 1968. Cambridge, Mass: MIT Press.

Hughes, T. (1967) *Poetry in the Making*. London: Faber.

Hughes, T. (1970) Myth and education. *Children's Literature in Education* 1 (1).

Jones, R. M. (1968) *Fantasy and Feeling in Education*. New York: New York University Press.

Koch, K. (1974) *Rose, Where Did You Get That Red?* New York: Vintage Books.

Martin, N. (1983) What happened to the stories? *Aspects of Education* (30). University of Hull.

Meek. M. (1982) *Learning to Read.* London: Bodley Head.

Meek, M. (1983) *Achieving Literacy.* London: Routledge & Kegan Paul.

Moffett, J. (1968) *Teaching the Universe of Discourse.* Boston: Houghton Mifflin.

Moon, C. (1984) Recent developments in the teaching of reading. *English in Education.* 18 (1).

Moss, E. (1977) 'The Peppermint Lesson'. In M. Meek, A. Warlow, and G. Barton (eds) *The Cool Web.* London: Bodley Head.

Moyle, D. (1982) *Children's Words.* Oxford: Blackwell.

Murdoch, I. (1977) *The Fire and the Sun.* Oxford: Oxford University Press.

National Library for the Handicapped Child (1986) *Catalogue of Library Holdings.* Available from the Library: Lynton House, 7–12 Tavistock Square, London WC1H 9LT.

Obrist, C. (1984) Extending reading outside the curriculum in the early years. *Reading* 18 (3).

Opie, I. and P. (1959) *The Lore and Language of Schoolchildren.* Oxford: Oxford University Press.

Ousby, J. (1980) Little factories of understanding. *Children's Literature in Education* 11 (4).

Paley, V. S. (1981) *Wally's Stories.* London: Harvard University Press.

Pringle, M. Kellmer (1974) *The Needs of Children.* London: Hutchinson.

Purves, A. C. and Beach, R. (1972) *Literature and the Reader.* Urbana, Ill: National Council of Teachers of English.

Quicke, J. (1985) *Disability in Modern Children's Fiction.* London: Croom Helm.

Rosen, H. (1983) *Stories and Meanings.* Sheffield: NATE Papers in Education.

Rosenblatt, L. M. (1970) *Literature as Exploration.* London: Heinemann.

Shapiro, J. E. (1979) 'Developing an awareness of attitudes'. In J. E. Shapiro (ed.) *Using Literature Affectively.* Newark: International Reading Association.

Smith, F. (1971) *Understanding Reading.* New York: Holt, Rinehart and Winston.

Smith, F. (1978) *Reading.* London: Heinemann.

Southgate, V., Arnold, H. and Johnson, S. (1981) *Extending Beginning Reading.* London: Heinemann Educational.

Teale, W. H. (1984) 'Reading to Young Children: Its Significance for Literary Development', In H. Goodman, A. Oberg and F. Smith (eds) *Awakening to Literacy.* London: Heinemann Educational.

Thomas, D. (1966) 'Notes on the art of poetry'. In J. Scully (ed.) *Modern Poets on Modern Poetry.* London: Collins.

Topping, K. and Wolfendale, S. (eds) (1985) *Parental Involvement in Children's Reading.* London: Croom Helm.

Vygotsky, L. S. (1962) *Thought and Language.* Cambridge, Mass: MIT Press.

Wade, B. (1982) Rhyming with reason. *Children's Literature in Education* 13 (4).

Wade, B. (1984) Story at home and school. *Educational Review Occasional Paper* 10. Birmingham: University of Birmingham.

Wade, B. and Moore, M. (1987) *Special Children, Special Needs*. London: Robert Royce.
Walsh, B. (1983) 'The basics and remedial English'. In B. T. Harrison (ed.) *English Studies 11–18: An Arts Based Approach*. London: Hodder and Stoughton.
Warnock, M. (1978) *Special Educational Needs*. London: HMSO.
Waterland, L. (1985) *Read with Me: An Apprenticeship Approach to Reading*. Stroud: The Thimble Press.
Wells, G. (1981) *Learning Through Interaction*. Cambridge: Cambridge University Press.
Wells, G. (ed.) (1985) *Language and Learning: An Interactional Perspective*. London: Falmer Press.
White, D. (1954) *Books Before Five*. New Zealand Council for Educational Research.
Williams, G. (1985) Learning to read through narrative in a special education class. *Gnosis* (7).
Wilson, M. D. (1983) *Stories for Disturbed Children*. Stratford: National Council for Special Education.

Children's books mentioned in the text

(Place of publication is London unless otherwise indicated.)
Adams, R. (1972) *Watership Down*. Rex Collings.
Agard, J. (1983) *I Din Do Nuttin and Other Poems*. Bodley Head.
Ahlberg, J. and A. (1977) *Burglar Bill*. Heinemann.
Ashley, B. (1981) *I'm Trying to Tell You*. Kestrel.
Berg, L. (1983) *Tales for Reading Aloud*. Methuen.
Brown, J. (1968) *Flat Stanley*. Methuen.
Byars, B. (1974) *The Eighteenth Emergency*. Bodley Head.
Cross, G. (1982) *The Demon Headmaster*. Oxford: Oxford University Press.
Heide, F. P. (1975) *The Shrinking of Treehorn*. Harmondsworth: Penguin.
Hoban, R. (1963) *Bedtime For Frances*. Faber.
Hoban, R. (1974) *How Tom Beat Captain Najork and His Hired Sportsmen*. Cape.
Hughes, T. (1968) *The Iron Man*. Faber.
Hughes, T. (1963) *How the Whale Became and Other Stories*. Faber.
Kemp, G. (1977) *The Turbulent Term of Tyke Tyler*. Faber.
McKee, D. (1980) *Not Now, Bernard*. Andersen Press.
Magorian, M. (1981) *Goodnight, Mr Tom*. Kestrel.
Marshall, A. (1974) *I Can Jump Puddles*. Harmondsworth: Puffin.
Oram, H. (1982) *Angry Arthur*. Andersen Press.
Ransome, A. (1930) *Swallows and Amazons* etc. Jonathan Cape.
Sendak, M. (1967) *Where the Wild Things Are*. Bodley Head.
Sewell, A. (1877) *Black Beauty*. Jarrold & Sons.
Southall, I. (1968) *Let the Balloon Go*. Methuen.
Sutton, E. (1973) *My Cat Likes to Hide in Boxes*. Hamish Hamilton.
Tolstoy, A. (1968) *The Great Big Enormous Turnip*. Heinemann.
Tomlinson, J. (1968) *The Owl Who was Afraid of the Dark*. Methuen.
Townson, S. (1982) *The Speckled Panic*. Andersen Press.
White, E. B. (1952) *Charlotte's Web*. Hamish Hamilton.
Wilder, L. I. (1937) *The Little House on the Prairie* etc. Methuen.
Wood, A. and Pilling, A. (1986) *Our Best Stories*. Hodder and Stoughton.

Name Index

Subject Index

Anthony Quinn was born in Liverpool in 1964. From 1998 to 2013 he was the film critic for the *Independent*. His novels include *The Rescue Man*, which won the 2009 Authors' Club Best First Novel Award; *Half of the Human Race*; *The Streets*, which was shortlisted for the 2013 Walter Scott Prize; *Curtain Call*, which was chosen for Waterstones and Mail on Sunday Book Clubs; *Freya*, a Radio 2 Book Club choice, and *Eureka*.

'A multi-character tale of a paranoid, dirty London at the tired end of the seventies' *Telegraph*

'Peopled by the kind of strong, fully realised individuals whom you could easily identify in a crowd, it is skilfully plotted and written with a rare elegance, sinuous wit and even optimism. It is a deeply satisfactory read' *Financial Times*

'Set during the dog days of the Callaghan Labour government, Anthony Quinn's latest period novel extends his richly pleasurable and loosely connected series portraying London down the decades' *Observer*

'[A] marvellous new novel ... This master storyteller recreates the whole world of the 70s, as the London we used to know is about to change for ever. The novel throbs with music and life, love and skulduggery, with the beating drum of the approaching Margaret Thatcher sounding the knell for that decade and the way we used to live on these islands' *i newspaper*

'Quinn is a witty and erudite writer who manages to make his characters' dialogue sound natural and engaging ... Quinn's book is a page-turning delight' *The Critic*